"A chapter on gun control is essential for dealing with Socialism Sucks. No gun control, no Socialism."

– Larry Pratt,
Executive Director Emeritus of Gun Owners of America (GOA)

"On national TV, Debbie Wasserman Schultz could not name a difference between Socialists and Democrats ... Many of us knew it to be a trick question at the time. The two merged years ago ... it is now a distinction without a difference."

– James Grisham,
Sean Hannity Show Producer

"In America, poor people are poor until they want more."

– Charles Butler,
Black Conservative Talk Show Host
(and Barack Obama's next-door neighbor)

SOCIALISM SUCKS
Your Money From Your Pocket

SOCIALISM SUCKS
Your Money From Your Pocket

JOE SIXPACK

Clovercroft Publishing

Socialism Sucks
Your Money From Your Pocket

Copyright ©2019 by Joe Sixpack Productions
All rights reserved.

Published by Clovercroft Publishing, Franklin, Tennessee

ISBN: 978-1-948484-96-1
Library of Congress Control Number: 2018955392

Printed in the United States of America

Dedicated to my kids, whom I love and of whom I am so proud;
free-thinkers and future six-pack drinkers (not Kool-Aid), all.

TABLE OF CONTENTS

THE SOCIALIST MENTALITY

SOCIALISTS LIE, CHEAT, AND STEAL

THE SOCIALIST STRATEGY

THE SOCIALIST ENDGAME

SOCIALISM SUCKS
Your Money From Your Pocket

INTRODUCTION

"So this is how liberty dies. With thunderous applause."
– Revenge of the Sith, 2005

Understanding Socialism is easy, really. When you boil it all down, it's on the wrong side of a battle between good and evil. What makes it worse is that Socialist leaders can get people to enthusiastically do their will by feeding them lies, like red meat to pit bulls.

In the Star Wars series, the "Empire" is ruled by an evil dark lord who controls his subjects with intimidation and fear; do what he says and you won't get hurt. He wants followers who do not think for themselves, only what he wants them to think. Anyone who is different must be destroyed. In the films, these free thinkers are represented by the Jedi.

Whatever or whoever the Empire can't control, it must destroy. Even in the films, the Empire is very similar to Nazis. The term "Stormtrooper" refers to Nazi soldiers. One look at the uniforms worn by Empire Commanders and it's very easy to see the resemblance to Nazi 'Brown Shirts'. Just do a *Google* search comparison and you will note the same style breeches (pants), jackboots and hats.

The Jedi are the underdogs. They are revolutionaries who seek freedom. They don't want to conform and become slaves; they want to think for themselves and be free (free thinkers). This is a spirit which exists in all of us. Perhaps that is one reason Star Wars has been so popular.

While it's widely acknowledged and obvious that Star Wars creator George Lucas modeled the Empire after the Nazis, something else about that is very interesting. The term "Nazi," when translated from German to English, means 'National Socialist Party.'

So, who is Joe Sixpack? He's not just a free thinker who authored this book. He also knows how to **stir the pot with common sense**. He speaks for a lot of people. You can bet that whenever he speaks, many heads will nod in agreement. Heads that shake in *disagreement* are usually Socialists.

Joe is the voice of many, maybe even you. If so, you contributed to writing this book when we brought Joe into the mix. That's why we recruited him. We wanted to include an author that says what so many people are thinking. We knew Joe could help us put those thoughts into words.

Another point of note when reading is that the terms "Democrat" and "Socialist" really mean the same thing today. As Hannity producer "Sweet Baby" James Grisham says, Socialists have found a home in the Democrat Party and have been shaping that Party to fit their needs for decades now.

The primary goal of this book is to pull back the curtain and show you the mentality of evil Socialists, how they act, how they plot to carry out their plans, what those plans are and where they lead.

Trust us, you want no part of where Socialism leads.

Just ask Joe.

SECTION I

THE SOCIALIST MENTALITY

CHAPTER 1

SOCIALISTS ARE AMONG US

"Socialism provides safety in numbers.
And that's OK, if you don't mind trading your name
—your identity and individualism—for a number."
– Jarod Kintz

Make no mistake about it; Socialism SUCKS! Not because we disagree with the philosophy behind it, though we most certainly do! It's because I have experienced first-hand, by living under Socialist regimes in Europe for a third of my life, where it ultimately leads ... and it's not pretty!

In the short-term, it feels good if you are a receiver—free stuff! Free money, free housing, free healthcare, free whatever. The problem with that is nothing in this world is free. There is no free lunch. Someone always must pay. Defenders of Socialism will say they are just fleecing the fat cats. Sounds good, right? Stick it to the man! Again, another problem. The "super-rich" strawmen Socialists claim to hate:

1

1) Don't have enough money to fund all the grandiose programs the Socialists want to push through, and ...
2) Are much smarter than the Socialists (proven by their acquisition of wealth) and can avoid having to pay more than they should.

The rub is that most of the wealth in this country is held by the middle-class, and this is what the Socialists are really after. They don't want to go after the big companies, even though they pretend they do. The real game is to rob the middle class of its wealth while at the same time, getting cozy with the big companies to share in their profits. By sucking the wealth from the hard-working middle class, the idea is to make the backbone of America dependent on the Socialists who run the government.

There is hope because a younger generation, Generation Z born between 1996-2010, is rejecting Socialism. A *New York Post* article by Salena Zito indicates that this generation is leaning conservative (right-wing) and rejecting left-wing or Socialist views. A big reason is that it's become harder for Socialists to push their lies because there is so much more information available.

A younger audience can sort through this information much more easily than previous generations. It's better equipped to discriminate between truth and lies. As the young members of this generation do so, they are finding that Socialism sucks and it is built on lies.

Socialism needs young minds. As such, it needs them to reject their parents and become dependent on the state. It seems to be losing there as well. Generation Z is showing greater respect for their parents and Socialists hate that!

"Gen Z actually like and trust their parents,
who have been transparent with them, much more than any generation before."
- Jeff Brauer, political science professor quoted by New York Post

Bill Ayers, a mentor to the most Socialist President in U.S. history, Barack Obama, once said:

"Kill all the rich people. Break up their cars and apartments.
Bring the revolution home, kill your parents, that's where it's really at."
– Bill Ayers

Dependence is the key to Socialism. Socialists know that if you are dependent on the State (getting "free" stuff), then you will always vote for the Socialists. Have you ever heard the phrase, "Don't bite the hand that feeds you"? That is how they sink their teeth in and lock their hold on power—by making as many people dependent on the state as possible. Once they have the majority locked in, they can do most of what they want. And make no mistake about it ...

They are going to do what is in their best interest, not yours.

Look no further back in history than the Soviet Union, which collapsed in 1991. The Socialists at the top lived like kings, drove around in Mercedes Benzes while the population lived on moldy cheese, stale bread, beer and vodka. If that sounds like the makings of a pretty good party, think again. It was a miserable existence, devoid of joy, accomplishment, innovation, and the bare necessities of life.

The goal of this book is to help you think for yourself instead of listening to "educators" and the major news outlets; accepting their interpretation of current events as the truth. They lie just as easily as any politician. As with anything in this life, if you want to understand what is really going on—as opposed to what people say is going on—follow the money-trail; that will lead to the truth. One outcome in a truly Socialist society is that the individuals of the population are unable to think independently. Common sense and critical thinking become lost.

Here is a fitting example of that:

Soon after moving to Europe in 2000, I was in an office building and one of the locks was jammed. The boss told the office manager to hit it with some WD-40. The office manager insisted that we needed a professional locksmith to handle the job. (In Europe, people don't "do-it-yourself" like we do here. They always call an electrician, plumber, whatever). Anyway, the locksmith shows up, looks at the lock, wisely scratches his beard, reaches into his bag, pulls out a can of WD-40 and squirts some into the lock. The total bill for charges was $150. Too funny! You can't make this stuff up. And this is just one of countless examples of the lack of reason and common sense that Socialism leads to. Funny? Yes, but when it's part of real life, it's very sinister.

Any government tends to move toward Socialism as it gets larger. Perhaps Ronald Reagan summed it up best when he said:

"Government is like a baby.
An alimentary canal with a big appetite at one end
and no sense of responsibility at the other."
– Ronald Reagan

As you read through this book, listen for that sucking sound and try to follow the common themes that run through the Socialist philosophy:

- It's OK to lie to achieve objectives by any means—ends justify the means.
- It's all about the money, dependency, and control.
- Projection: that is, accuse the other side of doing exactly what you are doing to put them on defense. After all, Socialists know what they're accusing their opponents of better than their opponents do (the Socialist already has the upper hand).
- We are all assumed to be too stupid to know what is good for us.
- Their sinister policies and programs always have warm, fuzzy names that disguise their true nature and make them more acceptable than they would otherwise be (see chapter 20 for examples).
- Urgency: When they want to do something, they always present it as an immediate crisis and create a false sense of urgency.

Ok, let's start exposing these control freaks!

CHAPTER 2

SEEING THE VISIBLE AND INVISIBLE HANDS

"Every individual ... neither intends to promote the public interest,
nor knows how much he is promoting it ...
he intends only his own gain, led by an invisible hand
to promote an end which was no part of his intention."
– Adam Smith

"As against the invisible hand of Adam Smith,
there has to be a visible hand of politicians whose objective is
to have the kind of society that is caring and humane."
– Pierre Trudeau

Perhaps no two quotes better express the difference between Capitalism and Socialism, or even good and evil. When people work hard and honestly, there are unintended consequences that are good for a society. This is what is known as the *Invisible Hand*, which does its *best* work when allowed to *do* its work—preferably, unimpeded by the visible hands of troublesome bureaucrats.

This is where the evil part comes in—the *Visible Hand*. In the quote above, former Canadian Prime Minister Pierre Trudeau (father of current Socialist Prime Minister Justin Trudeau) thought that government should take the wheel from the *Invisible Hand*—and drive. There are unintended consequences of this too. Socialists who promote this do so in the name of making everyone equal. What they're really doing is placing themselves above everyone else. It is the *Invisible Hand* which best promotes equality of opportunity and greater prosperity for all.

The worst that Capitalism has to offer is still preferable to the best of Socialism.

> *"The inherent vice of Capitalism is*
> *the unequal sharing of blessings.*
> *The inherent virtue of Socialism is*
> *the equal sharing of miseries."*
> *– Sir Winston Churchill*

In a very real sense, the *Invisible Hand* can be godly. If everyone does the *right* thing while earning a living, *good* things happen—and no one person gets the credit. When the *Visible Hand* spoken of by Trudeau takes the reigns, it leaves destruction in its wake and specific people are directly responsible for it.

However, those people will lie because the end justifies the means (breaking any rule, law or one of the Ten Commandments in the pursuit of something you want is perfectly ok) in their minds. What they want is power and if lying helps them get it, they'll do it; to them, it's war and war is about deceit. Perhaps the biggest reason people don't see the *Visible Hand* is because it's usually working behind your back or is in your pocket.

"...in war the end justifies almost any means."
– Saul Alinsky (see chapter 11)

The hand you *can't* see is largely productive and helpful to a society. The one you *can* see—if you so choose—is largely destructive and seeks to undermine society.

When a Socialist tells you he or she wants to use the government to help people, that person is either lying, ignorant, or both.

Career politicians exist to get elected, re-elected, and to spend money that isn't theirs, all in the name of helping people. They use the *Visible Hand* to reach into your pocket and steal from it. They'll call this "taxes" or even "investment" for the greater good; it's really just plain theft.

This is not to say taxes should be eliminated. They are needed for things like defending a nation, maintaining infrastructure, and keeping law and order. Unfortunately, politicians learned that they have great power and can get their hands on your money to make it theirs by telling you how much they care for the poor in society while adding new departments and bureaus that are rarely more than money pits. At some point, productive citizens became viewed as part of a "cash cow" that Socialists in government saw an opportunity to milk.

Socialists are people too (barely). As such, they fall victim to human nature just like anyone else. There comes a point when it's all about the money. That's the point where self-interest turns to greed. The more they get, the more they want. The more they want, the more lying, cheating, and stealing they are willing to do to get it. The Socialist who believes that the end justifies the means doesn't care how he acquires what he wants, only *that* he acquires it.

True Capitalism is when everyone pursues their individual self-interests honestly, with very limited government. Some people benefit more than others but everyone does benefit. True Socialism is when a powerful few are ruled by greed and everyone else suffers.

"Government that is big enough to give you everything you want is more likely to simply take everything you've got."
– Ronald Reagan

There are several common themes that run through the Socialist playbook, and they are usually very easy to spot if you know what you're looking for.

CHAPTER 3

AVOID THE BRAINWASHERS

"There are two ways to be fooled.
One is to believe what isn't true;
The other is to refuse to accept what is true."
– Soren Kierkegaard

Teenagers, what if we told you that you're fast-approaching an age when adults—many of them posing as college professors—will try to use your youth against you? They will attempt to brainwash you into believing lies. All the while, they'll be taking your money, putting you deep into debt and telling you how smart you are for believing them.

Would you believe *us*?

"No way," you say? "No one is gonna brainwash me. I'm my own person."

We hope you're right but bear in mind that today the list of people who *have* been deceived by brainwashers during their college years is endless ... and they don't even know it.

People of all ages want to be listened to, respected, and encouraged.

They don't want to be lectured; they want to be understood. They want to be taken seriously, not brushed off. Perhaps above all, they want to be dealt with honestly, not lied to.

If you're like most people, you don't want to play the fool.

Yet, that's what many colleges and universities do to their students these days and they *do* it by *pretending* to respect you, encourage you, listen to you, and tell you the truth. What most of them are *really* doing is exactly the opposite. And they know it damned well!

You may be deciding what you want to do after school. How many times do you get asked, "What do you want to do for a living?" or "Where are you going to go to school after you graduate?" or "What do you want to be when you grow up?" If you haven't decided, you're probably tired of being asked.

The truth about the college experience these days is that it has increasingly become an arm of government. As such, the brainwashers are pushing for America to adopt Socialism.

Socialism is a belief that no one really owns anything, that all possessions, wealth and means of production belong to the community. Sounds nice, huh? Everyone sharing and caring, right? That is how it is sold, but the brainwashers want exactly the opposite. What they *really* want is YOUR money! Socialism always leads to something much worse.

Vladimir Lenin was a communist revolutionary who was the early leader of Soviet Russia, a communist state that oversaw the murder of 50 million people by that government. Lenin himself knew that Socialism was just a means to communism.

> *"The goal of socialism is communism."*
> *– Vladimir Lenin*

The problem comes when Socialism is put into practice; it always fails. If everyone must share the wealth, someone or something must officiate the game, right? It should have unbiased referees, right? Someone or something must set the rules and implement them, right? For Socialism to even have a chance to work as it's sold to people, those who set and enforce the rules must be fair and not interested in owning wealth or possessions themselves.

Ah, but that is where they're given too much credit. In most cases, these people want what you have. In short, Socialism as it's sold is contrary to human nature. Socialists would have you believe that they are not driven by their own self-interests; that is another lie.

This is at the heart of what is known as the *Tragedy of Commons,* an economic theory of behavior. It says that individual self-interests always defeat the theory of contributing to the common good. The "common good" sounds great but always loses in the arena of reality.

If you're hungry, you will act in your self-interest to eat. If you're poor, you will act in your self-interest to break out of poverty. If you're low man on the totem pole, you will act in your self-interest and climb.

Whenever anyone tells you to set aside your own self-interests for the common good, you should always challenge that person. That person is either putting blind faith in a failed idea or is greedily seeking his own self-interest by expecting you to give up your private property. By setting aside your own self-interests, you are waving the white flag of surrender and putting cuffs on the invisible hand (see chapter 2).

What is often not considered is that understanding the *Tragedy of Commons* can lead to prosperity for all. In this survival of the fittest arena, the fittest often tend to help everyone around them do better.

> *"A rising tide lifts all boats."*
> *– President John F. Kennedy*

If you plan to go to college, just be mindful of the fact that the clear majority of ~~professors~~ brainwashers are pushing Socialism. It's much worse than it used to be because the federal government now runs the student loan programs. As always, follow the money. The college experience is being subsidized by the federal government more than ever before. Thus, the costs have gone up and the value of a college degree continues to go down in the real world.

That is what government does. The bigger it gets, the more destructive and incompetent it becomes.

> *"If you want more of something, subsidize it;*
> *if you want less of something, tax it."*
> *– Ronald Reagan*

For decades, young students have been told that if they want to get anywhere in life, they need a college degree. That may have been true but Socialists saw an opportunity to get in on the action. They've been hard at work, corrupting the college experience for generations now.

Today, there are simply far too many fields of study. The real opportunities exist for jobs in a trade (like electrician and plumber). These jobs are always in demand and pay more now because fewer and fewer people are qualified for them. If you're an electrician, you're likely to make more than many college graduates today.

If you want to become a doctor, a lawyer, an engineer, a business professional, an accountant, et al. the college experience makes sense. However, if you're interested in Puppetry, Transgender Studies, or Comedic Arts (all actual majors), you may want to reconsider. After all, if you're not funny, no amount of schooling is going to change that.

> *"Just because you're passionate about something*
> *doesn't mean you won't suck at it."*
> *– Mike Rowe*

Even as the cost of college goes up, graduates are less and less qualified to meet the needs of employers. What this means is that not only are many college degrees worthless—they stand as testaments to tuitional theft.

As Mike Rowe points out, there is a significant difference between following your passion and pursuing existing opportunities *with* passion. For example, if you're passionate about playing football, your opportunities are limited, but if you decide to pursue available opportunities *with* passion, you will find happiness instead of futility:

> *"Never follow your passion*
> *but always bring it with you."*
> *– Mike Rowe*

You see, Socialists want you to follow your passion without regard for what the market will pay. Why? Because they want you desperate and in debt. They can accomplish that with empty promises. That reality helps the Socialists, not you. The more you owe, the less pOWEr you have. That power is sucked up by the Socialists who now have you where they want you: fighting *for* them.

I encourage you to watch Rowe's video entitled, "Don't Follow Your Passion."

SOCIALISTS HATE AMERICA

If ever there were a country founded on anti-Socialist principles, it's the United States of America. Europeans who were fed up with government controlling their lives fled for better ones. They didn't *find* that better life; they found *opportunity* and *fought* for that better life.

It is no coincidence that American history is either not taught in schools today or it *is* taught from a Socialist, anti-American perspective. Students are told America was founded by imperialists who set out to steal land from the Indians. Schools rarely take the side of America's forefathers; they always seem to side with the Indians. They also choose to ignore the role of Great Britain's King George III, to whom the Declaration of Independence was addressed.

The British King was corrupt beyond measure. Here is a quote about King George from the Declaration that is always overlooked:

> *"He (King George III) has excited domestic insurrections amongst us,*
> *and has endeavoured to bring on the inhabitants of our frontiers,*

the merciless Indian savages, whose known rule of warfare
is an undistinguished destruction of all ages, sexes and conditions."

In America's founding documents, it wasn't the poor Indians who were the victims of colonialist oppression. It was the colonists who were victims of "savages" agitated by the King to be as barbaric as they could in fighting the King's disobedient subjects. This "agitation" is an important tactic of Socialists (see chapters 11 and 18). The colonists were trying to break free from the bonds of tyranny (government abuse of authority) and the tyrant showed just how ruthless he could be to those who rejected his rule in favor of freedom.

Yet, this perspective isn't taught in America's high schools or universities. Why? The answer is Socialism, which always leads to tyranny. Just look back at history for endless examples of this—Soviet Russia, Cuba, Venezuela, China, North Korea and even Nazi Germany (Nazi translated means National Socialist Party). The list goes on and on but those who push for Socialism always seem to get an audience for some reason.

"Those who cannot remember the past are condemned to repeat it."
– George Santayana

What's even worse when it comes to those who demand Socialism is that they cannot point to one example in which it has worked; it *always* fails.

CHAPTER 4

CASTLE THEORY

"Crouch down and lick the hands which feed you.
May your chains sit lightly upon you,
and may posterity forget that ye were our countrymen!"
– Samuel Adams

Less than one month after the Declaration of Independence was signed, forefather Samuel Adams delivered those words in a speech in Philadelphia to parliamentarians who wanted to stay loyal to the king. Adams isn't just famous for brewing beer (though he was very good at it). He was also one of America's early founders who was among the most determined to break free from England.

There is a reason for his passion and we refer to it as the Castle Theory. It goes like this.

The United States of America and Europe—while sharing a common origin—have evolved into two very distinct entities in terms of risk-taking and security. In other words, they are wusses and we are bad-asses!

Put yourself in the position of a typical European back at the end of the Middle Ages and the early stages of the Renaissance (roughly the year 1500 AD and forward). You live in a town or city in squalid conditions. At the center is a town square and the nobleman's castle. Towns and cities exist behind walls for protection. Outside the walls roam the thieves and highwaymen. You pay the king—indirectly through your local nobleman (pimp, pusher, whatever)—taxes in return for the protection he offers; you live as his subject.

You are not a free man; the king and noblemen rule as they please. The rule of law is what they say it is. They'd just as soon put your eye out with a hot poker for not paying your taxes. Oh, and they can set your taxes at whatever level they want. Complain and he might take out your other eye. Imagine that, no more hanging out on the corner ogling those eight maids a-milking.

After America was discovered, these people faced a choice. They could either remain where they were or—if they could afford to buy a place on a ship under extremely foul, overcrowded conditions—leave for America (at that time it was basically just a huge forest). If you were lucky enough to survive the journey (starvation, dysentery, cholera, scurvy—take your pick), you were then free to take your chances on your own against Indians (many were "merciless Indian savages"), bears, wildcats and wolves, as well as thieves and highwaymen.

Think about that. Stay where you are and trade your freedom for security or take a HUGE risk to you and your family for the opportunity (by no means guaranteed, or indeed, even probable). Take a huge risk on a low-probability outcome—that you and your family survive. If you do manage to survive, you then must feed, clothe and protect your family.

The people who took these risks wound up populating the United States. That is the stock of the American people: risk-takers. The Europeans are descended from the stock that chose to remain as the king's subjects in return for his (dubious) protection.

A similar case can be made for Australia and New Zealand, although in their cases those countries were founded as penal colonies so most of them were criminals. Maybe this helps explain why they are such fun, outgoing people. We've partied with Aussies and Kiwis. Those guys are crazy fun!

CHAPTER 5

A TALE OF TWO BUMS

"It is neither wealth nor splendor;
but tranquility and occupation
which give you happiness."
– Thomas Jefferson

That quote from America's third President is short but power-packed and oh, so true. Parts of human nature are very destructive. One such trait is the willingness to do nothing if someone else does the work. The human spirit, however, desires to be productive. Politicians love appealing to human nature instead of the human spirit, no matter how destructive it can be, because it gives them more power.

While a 16-year-old, I was sitting in a public park in Denmark drinking a beer (yes, in public, sixteen years old, and perfectly legal!). A seemingly able-bodied, working class guy of about 30 sat down next to me, only he had a case of beer (30 in Denmark), and proceeded to work his way through them. We got to chatting and I asked him what he did for a living. He replied that he didn't work.

"Well," I said, "how can you afford a full case of beer if you don't work?"

"I just got my monthly government check," he replied.

I asked him why he doesn't work. He looked at me as if I had two heads and asked, "Why should I work? If I work, I make DKK 3,000. If I don't work, I get DKK 2,700. So why should I work?"

He was right, we must admit. It was the system that was wrong, paying people not to work. The problem is that doing so only appeals to the worst in human nature:

> *"I've nurtured every sensation man has been inspired to have.*
> *I cared about what he wanted and I never judged him. Why?*
> *Because I never rejected him. In spite of all his imperfections,*
> *I'm a fan of man!"*
> *– Al Pacino as Lucifer in Devil's Advocate*

Fast forward twenty-odd years: I was late for a meeting in a U.S. city, dressed business casual and doing my best waiter's stride to get there quickly. As I approached a garbage can at full speed to deposit some piece of trash, a bum pushing his cart of "wares" approached the same garbage can. As we converged he said to me, "I can see you made it."

I tossed my trash and replied, "Not yet, but I'm working on it."

His reply to this shocked me a little. I was waiting—well, not really waiting, as I was cruising at top speed—for him to curse me out or hit me up for cash. Instead, as I powered along to my meeting, he shouted his reply to me.

"Right on, brother!"

I held up a clenched fist in reply and sped on my way with a renewed sense of shared spirit between myself and the bum. Two Americans going about their respective business who can have a brief, friendly exchange that does not seem possible today with either our ruling elite or with the useful idiots who've signed on as their foot-soldiers.

Right on brother, indeed!

The point of these two stories is two-fold. On the one hand, a system which encourages people not to work will lead precisely to that outcome;

able-bodied people sitting in the park drinking taxpayer-funded beer instead of working. You may think, "Woo-hoo!" and we might even agree, in theory. In practice, though, it kills the society just as surely as it will kill that poor, misguided fool; it robs him of his spirit and individualism.

On the other hand—and this speaks to the class warfare currently being waged by the Socialists in this country—you have the bum who is smarter than the Socialists. He's on his way for a mid-afternoon snack in the corner garbage can, sees a well-dressed person going about his business, and rather than demanding an entitlement as the Socialists would instruct him to do (attack the fat cats!), he calls out words of encouragement to a guy who is striving to "get it made." That's the American spirit, not taking down someone who is trying to get ahead and resenting him, but rather cheering him on.

God bless America!

SECTION II

SOCIALISTS LIE, CHEAT, AND STEAL

CHAPTER 6

WELFARE IS SICK

"Nobody spends somebody else's money as carefully as he spends his own.
Nobody has the same dedication to achieving somebody else's objectives
that he displays when he pursues his own."
- Milton Friedman

Nobel Laureate Milton Friedman delivered those words as part of his argument against welfare. When a government spends money on welfare, it is spending someone else's money—yours. As such, it is more careless with it than you would be.

A government taxing its citizens in the name of helping the poor is evil. The Socialist does this to appeal to your sense of decency while putting his hand in your pocket to steal from you.

Whenever you hear a Socialist talking about the use of tax dollars to subsidize caring for the country's poorest citizens, you should shout your opposition from the rooftops because you—and the poor—are about to be fleeced.

Consider Barack Obama, the 44th President of the United States. He ran on a campaign of "Hope and Change" while vowing to "transform" America. He had the overwhelming support of minority groups. The black population in America was thrilled that the country would have its first black president; his Socialist background was overlooked.

Under the Obama administration, black unemployment was the highest it had ever been. Welfare rolls, food stamps and the personal wealth of politicians exploded while the American middle class grew poorer. Despite this, the black population continued to hold Obama up as a great president. The racial divide in America became worse—instead of getting better—on Obama's watch.

Conversely, under Donald Trump—Obama's successor—black unemployment dropped to its lowest in recorded history, before Trump was in office for one year. Yet, blacks overwhelmingly hated Trump and loved Obama.

Why?

It's simple, really. To many, the *appeal* of Socialism is stronger than the evidence *against* it. There was also a loyalty many blacks had for Obama simply because ... he was black. Any time opponents disagreed with Obama, they were called racists. Nonetheless, reality *always* wins.

> *"The trouble with Socialism is that eventually*
> *you run out of other people's money."*
> *- Margaret Thatcher*

Known as the Iron Lady, Margaret Thatcher was the Prime Minister of Great Britain during the Cold War's later years. She also knew Socialism sucks. She embarrassed her Socialist counterparts with sound, simple arguments ... and a smile.

Toward the end of her time as Prime Minister, Thatcher was speaking in the House of Commons and was confronted by a Socialist Member of Parliament. After admitting that Thatcher had some "substantial success" with her policies, the politician then argued that under Thatcher, the "gap" between the richest and poorest of British citizens had grown.

Thatcher's response was a knockout punch. After pointing out that everyone was wealthier, Thatcher said of the politician's position:

> *"He would rather the poor were poorer*
> *provided the rich were less rich."*

Whenever a government claims it wants to be charitable, just remember it's spending someone else's money. When *individuals* (there's that term again) are given the opportunity to be generous with their *own* money, good things usually happen (see chapter 2). Individuals are more careful with their *own* money and spend it far more wisely than government.

When an individual decides to be charitable, the motive is most often pure—unless he's just using loopholes in the tax law (that'd be a great thing because it exposes government's incompetence). When a government tells you it is going to be charitable with the money it collects from others, it's nothing more than the best way to get people to part with it more easily.

In the Bible, the Gospel of John shows this perfectly. Chapter 12 begins with a description of Jesus having dinner at the house of Lazarus. Mary Magdalene anointed Jesus' feet with expensive perfume and wiped His feet with her hair. The perfume was Mary's *personal property* and she had chosen how to use it; that was not enough for Judas Iscariot:

4   But Judas Iscariot, one of his disciples (the one who was about to betray him), said,

5   "Why was this perfume not sold for three hundred denarii and the money given to the poor?"

6   (He said this not because he cared about the poor, but because *he was a thief; he kept the common purse and used to steal what was put into it.*)

7   Jesus said, "Leave her alone. She bought it so that she might keep it for the day of my burial." (John 12: 4-7).

Judas demonstrated Socialism in action, perfectly. Using deceit, he attempted to appeal to a sense of decency while really wanting to steal. Jesus clearly understood that the perfume was Mary's property and that she could do with it whatever she pleased. In fact, she found the *perfect* use for it.

Friedman also explained perfectly why he despised welfare. When the government takes more of your money, you have less of it with which to help others:

> *"One of the things I hold against the welfare system most seriously*
> *is that it has destroyed private charitable arrangements*
> *which are far more effective, far more compassionate, far more person to person*
> *in helping people who are really – for no fault of their own*
> *– in disadvantaged situations."*
> *– Milton Friedman*

When a government takes hard-earned money from its citizenry, it comes into possession of money it did not earn. It then re-distributes that money based not on the best use of it or even how the individual would spend it, but on how the government can benefit. An unsourced quote on the internet expresses the sentiment of welfare perfectly:

> *Over five thousand years ago, Moses said to the children of Israel*
> *"pick up your shovel, mount your asses and camels,*
> *and I will lead you to the Promised Land."*
> *Nearly 100 years ago, President Franklin Delano Roosevelt (a Democrat) said,*
> *"Lay down your shovels, sit on your asses, and light up a Camel,*
> *this is the Promised Land."*
> *Today, the government has stolen your shovel, taxed your asses, raised*
> *the price of Camels and mortgaged the Promised Land to China.*

True freedom does *not* come without hard work, and the promise of freedom *without* hard work always comes with strings attached that eventually become chains. Those strings include a dependent citizenry and an ever-growing government that seeks to slowly enslave its citizens through excessive taxation without true representation.

Once again, the Bible provides the answers. We refer you to 2 Thessalonians 3:10:

> *"For even when we were with you,*
> *we gave you this command:*
> *Anyone unwilling to work should not eat."*

That's going back quite a ways.

President Franklin Delano Roosevelt (FDR) argued that he could end poverty. Can you imagine a politician so arrogant to think he could eliminate poverty? Even Jesus said we will always have the poor among us. That makes FDR's claim even *more* arrogant. We've got a bunch of arrogant politicians in Washington, DC right now. Hell, you can't even spit in that town without hitting one.

Unfortunately for the American people—and the poor—any effort to eliminate poverty only benefits arrogant politicians, *not* the poor.

Roosevelt's idea was that people who choose not to work should be supported by the people who do. That doesn't sound like a very fair proposition, does it? Unless, of course, you are the one who has decided not to work (like the bum in Denmark). We've got a feeling the guy busting his back loading ships to feed his family would have a very different take on that; it would probably lead to him quitting. Why should he work for $100 when he can choose *not* to work and receive $75? That is where it leads.

If government pays people not to work, then people will oblige and not work in larger numbers than if the government didn't pay them at all. It's very simple.

People will work if the government ceases paying them *not* to.

Why? It's called survival. It is an instinct of man. Just as it keeps you from jumping off a high-rise, survival instinct drives you to work (along with your car or the bus driver).

As with almost everything it touches, government screws up through the Law of Unintended Consequences. On one hand, you have 535 members of Congress and the President. On the other hand, you have the collective intelligence of the entire country. Think about that—536 v. 300,000,000. Which team would you like to be on?

The answer can be seen in experiments where small and large groups are asked to estimate how many M&Ms there are in a mason jar. The larger group always comes closer than the smaller group. Why? Collective intelligence of the large group is always superior and more informed—and thus able to make better decisions.

The problem is that the politicians in Washington become so arrogant (there really must be something in the water in that town), that they really believe they are better able to make decisions on our behalf than are we. If there is anything more insane than that, we would love to hear it.

We refer you to the out-of-control national debt. It's those 536 people who are responsible for it, not the citizens whose money is being stolen and squandered in the name of God knows what. Yet, these elitists continue to encourage us to trust them. Another problem is that too many people just blindly do it, despite a mountain of examples that show they shouldn't.

Conservative icon William F. Buckley believed in the wisdom of the American people over arrogant elitists who look down their noses at the common man. He famously opined:

> *"I'd rather be governed by the first 2000 people*
> *in the Boston telephone directory than*
> *by the 2000 people on the faculty of Harvard University."*
> *– William F. Buckley*

The truth is that the very idea of government welfare is sick and demented. The "makers," who are largely charitable at heart, are taxed by their government to the point of having less with which to be charitable. The "takers" gladly take government subsistence (stolen money) and even *defend* said government against those from whom the government has stolen. Now *that* is sick. The government not only has newfound allies it has purchased with other people's money; it has also set up a slush fund for itself.

Government welfare is government sickfare.

CHAPTER 7

SOCIALIEZED MEDICINE

"I am going to try to re-organize (the healthcare system)
to be more amenable to treating sick people but that means you ...
young healthy people, you're going to have to pay more."
– Robert Reich

While speaking at the University of California at Berkeley, the Labor Secretary under Bill Clinton, Robert Reich, spoke those words to college students and was applauded. Reich led by saying he would deliver a speech that would reveal what a candidate for President "should say" about healthcare if he were being honest. He then suggested that children should let their parents die instead of caring for them (see chapter 1).

This too, was applauded.

If you think everyone in that room was mentally ill, you're mentally sane. College students—who were unable to avoid the brainwashers (see chapter 3)—were cheering the idea that they should pay more for health insurance with no increase in care while also allowing their parents to die.

That is sick.

Almost any time government seeks to insert itself into commerce—which is defined as economic activity (buying and selling of goods and services) between various parts of the country—just know that it is seeking to steal money. Using Reich's example, if young people are expected to pay more and their parents would be allowed to die rather than be saved, it means an increase in money from younger people and decreased costs from saving elderly people.

Someone is going to get that money. That someone is the sick Socialists in government.

SOCIAL SECURITY

Franklin Delano Roosevelt (FDR) and Lyndon Baines Johnson (LBJ) were among the most Socialist presidents in American history.

In 1935, FDR signed the Social Security Act, which laid the groundwork for social welfare in the United States. Publicly stated, its intent was to tax working Americans so that retired Americans who no longer worked could be paid a monthly income. The money would go into a "lockbox" and cared for by the trustworthy government. Who wouldn't want that?

That's how Socialists get what they want, by lying (remember Judas).

Do you honestly believe that government is going to take all that money from people and just lock it away for other people without taking a cut?

Not only have corrupt politicians taken their cut from social security, but that lockbox all the money is supposed to be in has been plundered. While that lockbox may not be empty, the money inside of it has been replaced with IOU's! There's no more money in it.

This is what happens when you trust Socialists:

> *"Because it has become increasingly difficult*
> *for individuals to build their own security single handed,*
> *government must now step in and help them lay the foundation stones."*
> *– FDR pushing social security*

Something Socialists are very good at is projection, which is the act of attributing to others, your own thoughts and beliefs. Socialists do this especially when the truth about what they believe is so ugly. Since they know it so well, they're good at describing it and blaming their opponents for holding those views. Those opponents then don't know how best to respond to the accusations.

During his re-election campaign of 1936, FDR mocked his opponents in a speech called 'Let Me Warn You' by pretending to verbalize their views. What he was really doing was verbalizing his own, especially when seeing what has happened to social security since. The worst part? It was totally predictable.

Later, in 1948, a cartoon was released entitled, "Make Mine Freedom," It shows exactly how the big government Socialists profit from promising things to all people. Then when things go bad with their programs, they will deny they were involved and work to solve a problem they themselves created. Granted, it is kind of hokey by today's standards but the message rings as true today as it did almost 70 years ago.

Yes, Social Security is broke because Socialists broke it. Today, debates about when the program will be insolvent (bankrupt) continue. Politicians—just like in the cartoon—will tell you "everything is fine," when it really isn't.

MEDICARE AND MEDICAID

Thirty years after the Social Security Act was signed by FDR, President Lyndon Baines Johnson (LBJ) signed the Social Security Amendments, which introduced Medicare and Medicaid into American culture. Since Social Security didn't address medical benefits, the Socialists found another way to scam the American people. LBJ didn't want the truth about how much Medicare would cost to be known.

"My health program yesterday runs $300 million,
but the fools had to go to projecting it down the road five or six years.
And when you project the first year, it runs $900 million…"
– LBJ on recorded phone call with Ted Kennedy

Medicare was presented as the government providing the elderly with health insurance and Medicaid as the government providing health insurance to the poor. They're bankrupt too. Don't listen to them when they tell you they're not. Socialists will use twisted logic to get you to believe everything is fine.

Socialists want you to believe they care for people, but that's only true if they're the only people we're talking about.

OBAMACARE

In 2010, the Barack Obama administration did to health care what FDR did to pass Social Security and what LBJ did to pass Medicare. Obama lied, lied some more, and then kept lying so he could pass the Patient Protection and Affordable Care Act (ACA / Obamacare).

We were told it would ensure that every American was *insured*. That's not what it was. It was another way for Socialists to sound good so they could steal from you. When clear-thinking Americans looked at the bill, logic dictated that it couldn't be paid for.

To get the bill passed, Obama had to assure people that their fears about losing their doctors or health care plans were unfounded.

Obama lied about this over and over and over. After the passage of Obamacare, many people *did* lose their plan and their doctor while their insurance costs skyrocketed.

There are countless videos of Obama promising people - multiple times - that they could keep their doctors and their plans. Many lost both.

During the Obamacare debate, Obama presided over a televised Health Care Summit. When it came time for Rep. Paul Ryan (R-WI) to speak, he called out Obama's plan as being full of "gimmicks and smoke and mirrors" right to the president's face. It was a face that conveyed it did not like being called out.

Some years after Obamacare was signed into law, a video surfaced of Jonathan Gruber, who helped to write the law. In this shocking discovery, Gruber spoke about the "stupidity" of the "American voter" and explained that the truth about Obamacare required its supporters to lie about it.

COST OF SOCIALIST LIES

Believing Socialist lies comes at great expense. The National debt sits at approximately $20 Trillion. Most people can't comprehend what even $1 Trillion looks like. You can do a google search and find several examples of people trying to explain it.

Imagine what $20 Trillion looks like. While you're busy trying to wrap your head around that, have a look at the national debt clock and take note of the Unfunded Liabilities figure. An unfunded liability is something that is owed but cannot be paid for without borrowing or having assets to pay for it. The unfunded liabilities number sits at well over $100 Trillion. Of that figure, Social Security and Medicare account for more than $45 Trillion.

http://www.usdebtclock.org/

So, what all this means is that Socialists like FDR, LBJ and Obama lied to the American people about *caring for* them, in order to *steal from* them—and YOU.

Doesn't that make you mad?

CHAPTER 8

SOCIALIST MEDIA

"The feeling most people get when they hear a Barack Obama speech ...
I felt this thrill going up my leg."
– Chris Matthews in 2008

"Well, that's a bitc h... Jesus ...
This is a different earth today than it was 24 hours ago."
– Chris Matthews on the night Donald Trump was elected

Political commentator Chris Matthews could not contain his gushing support for Barack Obama's candidacy in 2008. Nor could he contain his utter disgust for Donald Trump's candidacy in 2016. In each case, Matthews also wanted to be a respected newsman. Instead, he is one of the hundreds of living examples who demonstrate the suicide of objective journalism. The mainstream media (MSM) openly supported a Socialist president Obama and then showed open hatred for Trump; that is not objective.

Like all things Socialist, it's deceptive.

During one interview with President Obama, NBC news anchor Brian Williams literally bowed to Obama.

Years later, Williams—a supposedly respected, unbiased newsman—was exposed and disgraced as a serial liar. The lie that started unraveling his career was a story he told about being in a helicopter that was hit by an RPG while in Iraq. Each time he told the story, it grew. When called out by someone who was there, Williams had to come clean. The truth was that another helicopter traveling 30 minutes ahead of his, was hit. That prompted an investigation into how many other lies Williams told; they were many. Williams told these lies for ten years, with the knowledge of his network. Instead of being shamed out of the news business entirely, Williams was suspended and later added to the *MSNBC* lineup.

Another Socialist hero—Al Gore—had the support of the young Obama presidency when it came to pushing his climate change agenda. As such, Gore had the MSM on his side too. While doing an interview with CBS's *The Early Show* host, Harry Smith, Gore was encouraged to read aloud, a poem he wrote. Perhaps the only thing more embarrassing than the poem was Smith's reaction to hearing Gore recite it:

"Wow. I am so glad you read that. I'm happy to hear it in your voice."

The New York Times is so deceptive that it tries to show its objectivity by featuring a Socialist writer named David Brooks as a conservative (right-wing). Obama is arguably the most Socialist, left-wing president America has ever had. Yet, instead of challenging Obama, Brooks spent eight years fawning over him. In one article, Brooks expressed his feelings toward Obama:

"I remember distinctly an image of—we were sitting on his couches, and I was looking at his pant leg and his perfectly creased pant."
– New York Times *writer David Brooks on Obama in 2009*

During an appearance on the Tim Russert show after Obama was elected, Brooks praised Obama:

> I would write these columns attacking the Republican Congress but just to make myself feel better, I would throw in a few sentences attacking Democrats. And Obama sent me an email one morning and it said, 'David, if you want to attack us, fine, but you're throwing in those sentences to make yourself feel better' ... It was like he read my mind, better than I could. And that's the level of perceptiveness that he has.

As much as the MSM exposed its true self during the Obama years, it did so even more during the campaign and presidency of Donald Trump. MSM hatred for Trump dominated the news cycles. To the degree it allowed Obama to go unchallenged, the MSM never stopped going after Trump.

Shortly after Trump was inaugurated he held a news conference—filled with MSM reporters—and called them out for being "out of control" and "totally dishonest."

CNN BECOMES TRUMP'S BIGGEST TARGET

While Trump took issue with several "news outlets," *CNN* seemed to be at the top of the list. The term "Fake News" was introduced by Socialists to attack right-wing news outlets. However, Trump managed to take the term and apply it directly to *CNN*. For months after he became president, the Socialist media was obsessed with lying about a connection between Trump and Russia, without any evidence. That didn't stop them from pushing the story.

As time went on, Trump kept being proven right. At one point three *CNN* journalists were forced to resign after having to retract a false and negative story about Trump and Russia.

Soon thereafter, a series of undercover videos were released by *Project Veritas*. In them, various *CNN* employees were caught red-handed. A *CNN* editor admits that the connections between Trump and Russia were "bull**it."

The second video to be released showed Van Jones—an avowed Communist that *CNN* has been trying to make respectable—admitting that the Trump and Russia story is a "big nothing burger."

In the next video that was released, another *CNN* producer was caught admitting complete bias toward Trump. When asked if his network was "impartial," the producer responded, "in theory" right before he said all his colleagues recognize Trump is "a clown." Again, the biggest problem with the Socialists of the mainstream media is not that they're Socialists. It's that they pretend to be objective while *being* Socialists. It's grand scale lying.

Trump continued to respond via twitter to what he perceived to be unwarranted attacks. He engaged the media in ways Republicans had never done before; he got in the mud with the media.

The real irony is that the media ridiculed Trump by suggesting he should "run the country" instead of tweeting about the media. The reality is it likely took Trump less than five minutes to post the tweet. Yet, it was the media that talked about it 24/7.

SOCIALIST MEDIA EXPOSED BY WIKILEAKS

In the weeks prior to Trump's election in 2016, *WikiLeaks* released thousands of emails to and from far left-wing, Socialist Democrat John Podesta. Among other things, those emails revealed nearly 70 "objective" journalists who were actively working with the Democrat party to help Hillary Clinton get elected.

One of those reporters was George Stephanopoulos. During the Bill Clinton administration, Stephanopoulos was a key figure in the Clinton "war room." He even admitted to intimidating women into silence who had accused Clinton of sexual assault. Today, Stephanopoulos is the anchor of *ABC's This Week,* a Sunday morning show that is supposed to be moderated by an un-biased host.

During the Trump campaign, it was learned that Stephanopoulos contributed $75,000 to the Clinton Foundation and never disclosed it. When the news became public and something Stephanopoulos could no longer ignore, he had to address it on television. While admitting he was wrong, Stephanopoulos insisted he did it to help AIDS victims and children (a typical Socialist tactic).

Later, in an interview with Trump, Stephanopoulos asked the Republican nominee about things he might regret. Instead of falling for the game of Socialist "gotcha," Trump told Stephanopoulos he was sure the ex-Clinton war room guy regretted contributing that $75,000. Stephanopoulos was visibly uncomfortable at being called out.

Soon after being elected President in 1993, Bill Clinton fired all 93 U.S. Attorneys. There was barely a peep from the media about it. Then in 2007, Republican George W. Bush fired seven U.S. Attorneys and the media treated it like it was a major scandal.

Consider a more recent example courtesy of *POLITICO* (another left-wing publication posing as an objective one). Soon after Donald Trump was elected president, 46 U.S. Attorneys were asked to resign. *POLITICO* writer Josh Gerstein's headline read, "Trump team ousts Obama-appointed U.S. attorneys." Yet, when Barack Obama did the same thing after his election, Gerstein's headline read, "Obama to replace U.S. Attorneys," as if Obama had nothing to do with creating the vacancies.

To lie like they do, Socialists must believe their own lies. Case in point is far left-wing *MSNBC* Socialist commentator Rachel Maddow. During an appearance on *Real Time with Bill Maher,* Maddow stated that her job was to present the news, not give her opinion. The reality is that Maddow is a Socialist who pushes her ideology 24/7. That she believes otherwise is a testament to just how evil Socialism really is.

> *"Listen, my job is to cover these things,*
> *not to tell you how I like them or not."*
> *– Rachel Maddow, 2012*

America's founding fathers knew the importance of a free press (media). That's why they put it in the first amendment to the Constitution.

They knew that as a government becomes corrupt, it desperately needs a media (press) that won't oppose it, at least not too much.

Somewhere along the line, the MSM became an *arm* of government establishment and Socialists. It did so gradually, over time; it also did so through deceit. What the media needed most to carry out that deceit was a perception that it was objective. After all, if the media is objective, it's telling you the unvarnished truth, without emotion. As such, you shouldn't challenge it (when Socialists have your trust, they have everything).

The problem is that Socialists in the media simply wanted to create the *perception* that news—whether digital, in print, television or radio—was objective. Once it did that, it could own the news and push its Socialist agenda more easily. Walter Cronkite was a newscaster known as "the most trusted man in America" during the Vietnam War, despite having a Socialist, globalist agenda that he revealed publicly after his retirement (see chapter 18).

Take any mainstream media source you want. *The New York Times, Washington Post, ABC, NBC, CBS, CNN, USA Today, Associated Press, Reuters,* et al. Each one of these outlets claims to be objective. That is a lie (remember, that's what Socialists do). It's also important to remember that the Democratic Party has increasingly become more and more Socialist over the years. That is why it should come as no surprise that members of the mainstream media are overwhelmingly Democrats (Socialists).

CHAPTER 9

MULTI-CULTURALISM IS RACIST—CALL IT OUT!

"I want to go to a place where the minorities
don't outnumber the majority."
– Archie Bunker

The smallest minority on planet earth is the individual. If you believe—as we do—that every individual is unique and deserving of "certain unalienable human rights" then the individual is the tiniest of *all* minorities. In fact, as the earth approaches a population of 10 billion people, the individual is outnumbered beyond measure.

Now *that* is someone who needs defending!

Those who do not consider the rights of the individual before the rights of minority groups are the ones who are racist. If individual members of a *majority* group are discriminated against in the name of defending the rights of a minority group, isn't that being racist against the smallest of minorities?

It's also called bullying and the Socialists do it not out of concern for minorities. They do it to enrich themselves. Think of cockfighting. This is a blood sport in which two roosters are intentionally pitted against one another. Spectators sit back and watch the roosters fight to the death after placing their bets.

In a very tangible way, this is what Socialists do. Instead of roosters, they like to do it with people. While they don't get people to fight to the death, Socialists *do* seek to create sides. They then sit back and watch as those sides serve the Socialist's interests by fighting one another instead of identifying Socialists as the problem. Again, this is not a new concept; it's been going on for years (see chapter 7).

Multiculturalism leads to division. What? I thought multicultural-ism was about *embracing* diversity, you say? Nonsense. Before political correctness we had Americans, period. With multiculturalism, they have created hyphenated Americans: African-Americans, Muslim-Americans, Hispanic-Americans, Asian-Americans, *ad infinitum, ad nauseam!*

You are either American or you are not. Socialists have this weird urge to rule and regulate EVERYTHING. They love to pit people against each other. Have you ever heard of the old strategy of ruling called Divide and Conquer? By separating people into groups, Socialists seek to pit them against each other and the government can push through even more rules and regulations to rule and regulate the groups they created. Sound crazy? It is, but unfortunately it is also highly effective.

It's called class warfare and it's very dangerous. Socialists don't care because when people turn violent, as they often do in these matters, the guys who pushed these policies on the rest of us will be sitting up on Capitol Hill or in the manor house, having their stuffed goose, safe from the dangerous consequences of their intentionally idiotic policies.

The beauty—from their point of view—is that once everything is cat-egorized, they have all kinds of combinations they can pit against each other: Rich-poor, black-white, black-Mexican, white-yellow. Hell, if we start mixing bits of each group with bits of other groups we could end up with more colors than a box of Crayola crayons. Wait a minute, that's what America was before these Socialists started putting us into groups so that we could be regulated. So, are they trying to create what was already there? Not quite. They want us to identify with interest groups, NOT with the country.

It's easier to control us that way.

Bad people come in all sizes, shapes, and colors—black, white, yellow, brown, fat, short, tall, skinny. We don't discriminate based on color or anything else, we hate 'em all. Ditto for liking the good ones.

You're probably familiar with the saying, "When in Rome, do as the Romans do." The message is simple. You should honor the culture of your host country. Socialists in America want you to do the opposite. They want you to give up your culture to that of foreigners who are in your country already. Then they call it racist if you demand that such foreigners assimilate or become a part of your country.

To paraphrase comedian Jeff Foxworthy, if you fall for multi-culturalism, you might be a racist.

CHAPTER 10

BLACK DECEPTION

"I'll have those niggers voting Democratic for 200 years."
– Attributed to President Lyndon Baines Johnson (LBJ)

LBJ was a Socialist Democrat. He also signed the Civil Rights Act of 1965 into law. The quote above has been attributed to him by two individuals who heard him say it. That quote lives on because there is no better explanation for why blacks overwhelmingly support the Democratic Party. Since LBJ, black support of the Democratic Party has consistently been at about 90 percent. This is perhaps the greatest deception in American history.

Why?

The Democratic Party is the party of the mass murder of black babies (abortion), slavery, and racism. So how does the party continue to get away with this deception? That answer can be illustrated by the Rope and Ladder Theory (RLT), which states:

*"Blacks are in a hole. Instead of giving them a ladder,
Democrats throw them a rope and pull them
up half way, leaving them dependent on Socialism."*

Another destructive trait of human nature is the tendency to take the path of least resistance; water does this. Water will always flow to the lowest point. When it comes to flowing water, movement occurs with zero effort. Yes, it's always moving forward (a term Socialists love to use) but it's always going downhill.

Go figure. Human beings are comprised mostly of water!

Socialists exploit this trait as well and they have been doing so with blacks for decades.

In human nature, when minimal effort is rewarded, so are those who do the rewarding (see chapter 5). In the case of Democrats, they are rewarded for pretending to care about blacks in return for black votes.

But wasn't Abraham Lincoln, the President who fought against slavery, a Republican?

Yes.

So how do Democrats defend their Party, which founded the Ku Klux Klan (KKK)? Well, if you bring that up to a Democrat, what you will most likely hear is that the Republican and Democratic Parties switched sides at some point in history. They will tell you that the Democrat beliefs of today were the Republican beliefs at the time of the civil war.

The truth is that the only thing the Democrats switched was their tactics.

The 13th amendment to the U.S. Constitution was ratified on December 6, 1865; it abolished slavery. Republicans were responsible for ratifying it. Less than three weeks later—on Christmas Eve—the KKK was formed as the armed wing of the Democratic Party. Their charter was to persecute, terrorize, torture and murder blacks who had been freed.

Five years later, the 15th amendment was ratified. This gave blacks the right to vote. Again, Republicans are to thank. The KKK upped its game. It couldn't have blacks voting against the Democratic Party. The KKK then threatened blacks with physical harm if they voted Republican. As time passed, this became much more difficult to accomplish.

At some point, Democrats adopted the message of an old Italian proverb:

"You can catch more bees with honey than with vinegar."
– Giovanni Torriano 1666

There were two points in time during the 20th century when Democrats picked up a considerable number of black votes. The first was in 1936, during the re-election of Franklin Delano Roosevelt (FDR), when the sitting Democrat President received 71 percent of the black vote. Remember, FDR said he could end poverty and signed the very Socialist Social Security Act of 1935 one year earlier.

Yet, FDR also supported the KKK. In fact, he nominated a KKK leader to the U.S. Supreme Court named Hugo Black in 1937.

Black spoke publicly about his KKK membership during a 1937 radio address. In it, he admitted to being a member of the KKK but attempted to diminish that role.

The second point when Democrats picked up an increase in black votes was in 1964, when President Lyndon Baines Johnson (LBJ) received a whopping 94 percent of the black vote (See the LBJ quote at the beginning of this chapter). That year, Johnson helped to push through the Civil Rights Act of 1964. Since that time, blacks have over-whelmingly voted Democrat.

LBJ also took the baton from FDR when it came to Socialist government programs.

OPPORTUNITY LOST (OR AVOIDED)

One year after LBJ was elected, his labor Secretary Daniel Patrick Moynihan wrote a long report on the condition of blacks. The civil rights of blacks was a big issue at the time. Moynihan saw the destruction of the black family as something that needed fixing.

"The Negro family in the urban ghettos is crumbling."
– Daniel Patrick Moynihan, 1965

In the more than 50 years since, what's changed? Since LBJ helped guarantee the black vote for the Democrats for decades to come, the problem identified by Moynihan has either not changed or has gotten worse. LBJ backed away from Moynihan's report when many in the black community chose to reject it. Their reason for rejecting it should be a source of intense study.

Moynihan's message was that despite civil rights legislation, if blacks were to have better lives, the answer lay in re-building the family unit. While the black race in America had been victims of slavery, the solution was not to be found in remaining victims. Yet, this is what many Democratic politicians seized upon—and have for years.

VICTIMOLOGY

As the years passed, black leaders like Jesse Jackson and Al Sharpton learned how to make money using the rope and ladder theory. As Democrat politicians guaranteed black support by pulling them up halfway, people like Sharpton and Jackson just kept telling blacks they were being kept down.

They just didn't reveal who was responsible—the Socialists. In Congress, many of those Socialists are black. Consider the Congressional Black Caucus (CBC), which is clearly a racial group (you won't ever see the Congressional White Caucus).

The CBC also capitalizes on matters of race. Instead of solving real problems in the black community, the CBC follows the rope and ladder theory as well—on its own race. The reason is both sick and simple. They tell blacks that it's the Republicans who are responsible for keeping them down. In reality, members of the CBC are doing the bidding of Socialists—against their own race!

In 2009, it was learned that 70 members of Congress belonged to the Democratic Socialists of America (DSA) caucus. More than 70 percent of the CBC members were found to be in that caucus. Several years earlier, a black Republican and former Oklahoma Sooner quarterback J.C. Watts was elected to Congress. He rejected the CBC and when asked about his decision not to become a member, said this:

> *"They said that I had sold out and (am an) Uncle Tom.*
> *And I said well, they deserve to have that view.*
> *But I have my thoughts. And I think they're race-hustling poverty pimps."*
> *– J.C. Watts, 1997*

Again, Socialists in America may have committed their greatest deception by getting blacks to support them in overwhelming numbers.

SECTION III

THE SOCIALIST STRATEGY

CHAPTER 11

COMMUNITY ORGANISMS

"Lest we forget at least an over-the-shoulder acknowledgment to the very first radical:
from all our legends, mythology, and history ...
the first radical known to man who rebelled against the establishment
and did it so effectively that he at least won his own kingdom — Lucifer."
– Saul Alinsky

Left-wing Socialists seem to revere Satan (see chapter 18). In this case, it's Saul Alinsky, a hero to the most Socialist president in U.S. history, Barack Obama. Hillary Clinton, the Socialist woman who nearly became president after Obama, was also a huge fan of Alinsky; she wrote her Senior College thesis about him. Alinsky also revered her.

Who was Alinsky?

He's known as the founder of modern-day community organizing.

Ok, so what is community organizing?

Well, like all things Socialist, the term is intended to sound good but it's not at all. Alinsky believed in appealing to the worst of human nature.

"The despair is there;
now it's up to us to go in and rub raw the sores of discontent,
galvanize them for radical social change."
- Saul Alinsky

Not a very uplifting message, is it? Alinsky believed in "social change" by making people—many of whom were receiving government benefits—believe they were victims of injustice. In fact, that bum in Denmark (See chapter 5) would have been a perfect candidate. After all, he had nothing better to do, right?

Alinsky believed in picking an issue such people could relate to, then fanning the flames of anger, and pouring gasoline on it. Groups of angry people were formed who would then intimidate others until they backed down (Just like what King George tried to do with the Indians).

It's nothing more than creating angry, mindless mobs that thrive on bullying.

Alinsky is best known for his book, Rules for Radicals, published in 1971. In it, Alinsky presented his rules on how to stir up people into hateful, frenzied mobs and then organize. More than a half century earlier, Christian pastor William J.H. Boetcker produced the *Ten Cannots*, which clearly represent the exact opposite. Boetcker *focused* on the individual while Alinsky sought to *target* individuals and sic angry mobs on them (see chapter 9).

At the 1992 Republican National Convention, Ronald Reagan referred to Boetcker's "Cannots" in his speech, though he incorrectly credited Abraham Lincoln.

Here they are:

1. You cannot bring about prosperity by discouraging thrift.
2. You cannot strengthen the weak by weakening the strong.
3. You cannot help little men by tearing down big men.
4. You cannot lift the wage earner by pulling down the wage payer.
5. You cannot help the poor by destroying the rich.
6. You cannot establish sound security on borrowed money.
7. You cannot further the brotherhood of man by inciting class hatred.

8. You cannot keep out of trouble by spending more than you earn.
9. You cannot build character and courage by destroying men's initiative and independence.
10. And you cannot help men permanently by doing for them what they can and should do for themselves.

Contrast those ten truths with Alinsky's rules. Notice how he focused on deceit, bullying and intimidation. After reading these rules, you may be able to see why he dedicated his book to Lucifer. Here they are (emphasis ours):

1. Power is not only what you have, but what an opponent thinks you have. If your organization is small, *hide* your numbers *in the dark* and raise a din that will make everyone think you have many more people than you do.
2. Never go outside the experience of your people. The result is *confusion, fear, and retreat.*
3. Whenever possible, go outside the experience of an opponent. Here you want to cause *confusion, fear, and retreat.*
4. Make opponents live up to their own book of rules. "You can kill them with this, for they can no more obey their own rules than the Christian church can live up to Christianity."
5. *Ridicule* is man's most potent weapon. It's hard to counterattack ridicule, and it infuriates the opposition, which then reacts to your advantage.
6. A good tactic is one your people enjoy. "If your people aren't having a ball doing it, there is something very wrong with the tactic."
7. A tactic that drags on for too long becomes a drag. Commitment may become ritualistic as people turn to other issues.
8. Keep the pressure on. Use different tactics and actions and use all events of the period for your purpose. "The major premise for tactics is the development of operations that will maintain a *constant pressure upon the opposition*. It is this that will cause the opposition

to react to your advantage."

9. The **threat** is more **terrifying** than the thing itself.

10. The price of a successful attack is a constructive alternative. Avoid being trapped by an opponent or an interviewer who says, "Okay, what would you do?"

11. **Pick the target, freeze it, personalize it, polarize it.** Don't try to attack abstract corporations or bureaucracies. **Identify a responsible individual.** Ignore attempts to shift or spread the blame.

Obama was not only a student of Alinsky; he used what he learned throughout his presidency. His actions indicated he rejected all Boetcker's cannots, as evidenced by his dislike for Reagan. In a debate with Hillary Clinton, Obama let the truth slip out:

"I've spent a lifetime fighting against Ronald Reagan's policies."
– Barack Obama, 1/21/08

Community organisms are comprised of brainwashed individuals who serve the interests of others who seek to use them.

CHAPTER 12

COMMUNIONISM

"Your agenda has been my agenda in the United States Senate."
– Barack Obama to Service Employees International Union, 2007

The Service Employees International Union (SEIU) is a group that represents government employees and healthcare workers. The overwhelming majority of these workers vote for Democrats. Shortly after Barack Obama took office in 2009, he helped ram through a $787 billion stimulus package that was named the American Recovery and Reinvestment Act (ARRA). The stated purpose was to help create jobs—to "stimulate" the economy.

That's not what happened and that was not the intent (remember, Socialists lie).

So what was the Stimulus Package?

The answer is simple. It was nothing more than a money laundering scheme. The most basic definition of money laundering—which is a crime—is to make "dirty money" appear "clean." In this case, the Stimulus

Package took nearly $1 billion of taxpayer dollars, most of which belonged to people who didn't support Obama or Socialism, and gave a lot of it to groups like the SEIU. In turn, these groups donated a sizable portion of those dollars to help get Democrats elected.

> *"It (Stimulus Package) was a money laundering operation,*
> *as is all of public sector union employment."*
> *– Rush Limbaugh, 2011*

As has been the case with Socialists in the U.S. government for more than 100 years, American taxpayer dollars were stolen by those Socialists and used *against* those taxpayers. Unfortunately, it's largely done in such a way that it goes unnoticed. Socialists have the mainstream media on their side (see chapter 8) and most taxpayers are too busy to pay attention. Throw in a bit of money laundering and the theft is complete.

Days before the Stimulus was passed, Obama mocked his critics, saying to a group of Socialist Democrats who were frothing at the mouth for those taxpayer dollars:

> *"Then you get the argument,*
> *'this is not a stimulus bill; this is a spending bill'...*
> *What do you think a stimulus is?!*
> *That's the whole point!"*
> *– Barack Obama, February 5, 2009*

Of course, that wasn't the argument posed by Obama's opponents at all. The argument had to do with where the money was coming from, whose money it was and how it was going to be spent. The money was being stolen from taxpayers who objected and had no real representation in Congress. Worse, a huge portion of it was given to unions whose work very much included electing Democrats.

"Taxation without representation is tyranny."
– James Otis, 1761

One of the catchphrases used by the Obama administration to help justify the Stimulus Package was that it would create "shovel ready" jobs. But as the months came and went, Obama was forced to admit the truth. Unemployment continued to rise and economic growth continued to slow.

"Shovel ready was not as ... uh ...
shovel ready as we expected."
– Barack Obama, June 13, 2011

Obama made that statement at a White House Jobs Council meeting and did so in a joking manner. Imagine, the man responsible for stealing taxpayer dollars to gain more power and to intentionally hurt those from whom he stole, laughed about it. Again, Socialists are sick.

Meanwhile, the money that was supposed to help everyone was going to political causes and campaigns to elect the same Socialists who stole that money.

UNIONS AND HEALTHCARE

The Patient Protection and Affordable Care Act (ACA / Obamacare) had the full support of SEIU and the Community Organisms like the Association of Community Organizers for Reform Now (ACORN). The largest labor federation in the U.S., the American Federation of Labor - Congress of Industrial Organizations (AFL-CIO) also supported Obamacare.

As is the case with all Socialist enterprises, the leaders of these unions seek to enrich themselves while *pretending* to care for others. They are experts at employing the Rope and Ladder Theory as well (see chapter 10). In exchange for empty promises, their members blame those not responsible for keeping them down. As a result, they keep *themselves* down.

The healthcare debate of 2009-2010 was *not* about going after those rich insurance companies, but that's what the American people were told. The real aim of Obamacare was to put the government in charge of healthcare. The Socialists in power knew, though, that they couldn't just push through a bill that gave government total control. It had to be done in steps. It's why Socialists prefer to be called "progressives." With Socialists, it's all about moving forward—with evil.

> *"The objective is what's important, not the means."*
> *— Rahm Emanuel, June 17, 2009*

At the time Emanuel made that statement, he was Obama's chief of staff. The objective he referred to was "single payer," which means that all healthcare services would be run by the government. This is central to what Socialism is about—taking private industries and making them government-run. The unions knew that the $787 billion stimulus package would eventually run out. Single payer would give the government—and the unions—a steady stream of income.

Why?

Because everyone needs healthcare and if the government gets a cut of everyone's healthcare expenses, so will the unions. Those unions will then do with their cut what they did with their cut of the stimulus—launder it and then spend it on getting Socialist Democrats elected.

In 2003—a full five years before he was elected President—Obama spoke at an AFL-CIO Conference on "Civil, Human and Women's Rights" (See chapter 20) and said this in a video that was uncovered in 2008.

> *"I happen to be a proponent of a single-payer, universal healthcare plan."*
> *— Barack Obama, 2003*

In an interview with the *NBC* Today show, Obama was confronted with that video alongside remarks he made at a debate about never having supported a single-payer system. He then said he couldn't hear the 2003 audio and proceeded to lie his face off.

THE UNION MENTALITY

One person we spoke to who is experienced in dealing with unions referred to them this way:

"Unions are made up of unproductive obstructionists who get nothing done and prevent others from getting things done."

When asked why they do this, the former manager at a unionized company in Detroit said, "They think they're saving their jobs."

He went on to confirm that union bosses—whether in government or in corporate America—demand that no one think for themselves. Anyone who objects to the union's ways is targeted, isolated, and intimidated until they get back in line. You will note that this is exactly what Saul Alinsky taught (See Introduction about Star Wars).

The union mentality—especially among union bosses—is about bullying. Union workers are required to pay union dues; they have no choice. What they get in return is a demand for compliance. Thinking for oneself is forbidden. As for the union bosses, it's about control. The workers are bargaining chips. The more chips bosses have, the more money and power they can get. This is what "collective bargaining" is all about. It's a term used to describe negotiations between workers and management over things like wages, benefits, and conditions.

Unfortunately for the workers, it's a recipe for disaster. Consider the auto industry. Over the years and after several collective bargaining agreements, workers were awarded pensions and bonuses that companies couldn't pay. Selling cars at higher prices was a short-term option, but the Japanese eventually sold better quality vehicles at lower prices. This is how the invisible hand works (see chapter 2).

At a campaign rally for the re-election of Barack Obama in 2011, James P. Hoffa, Jr., President of the International Brotherhood of Teamsters Union, shouted about the anti-Socialist Tea Party:

"Let's take these son of a bitches out!"
– James P. Hoffa, Jr.

Union leaders have a Socialist mentality. They want to use people to enrich themselves. They want to destroy the free market. They seek to enrich government and destroy the private sector. They seek to exploit, intimidate, and threaten. Just as Socialists do, unions seek government control of industry.

That is what makes them CommUNIONists.

CHAPTER 13

NOTHING LEFT BUT VIOLENCE

"The Democratic Party loves mob uprisings. It's their path to power."
– Ann Coulter, 2011

Socialists want you to believe that Republicans, conservatives, and Christians are racist and violent toward anyone not like them. The truth is exactly the opposite (again). Just look at any violent movement. Odds are well over 95 percent that it's rooted in Socialism and supports Democrats or Islam (see chapter 19).

Instances of Christians committing violence are so rare that the Socialists must make things up. For example, Timothy McVeigh was found guilty of detonating a bomb in Oklahoma City in 1995 that murdered 168 people. Today, whenever you ask a Socialist for an example of a Christian terrorist, they love to include McVeigh.

There is one problem. Before he was executed, McVeigh told his biographers that he was "agnostic" and that he considered "science" to be his religion (think man-made climate change (see chapter 17)).

In many cases, Democrat operatives commit fake crimes themselves and try to frame their opponents. The examples are endless. Again, this is also anti-Christian. It's called bearing false witness (Socialists love violating the Ten Commandments).

The modern-day violence from the left can be traced back to the 1960s. Left-wing groups sprung up on college campuses across the country. One such group was the Students for a Democratic Society (SDS). A terrorist named Bill Ayers broke away from this group because he thought it wasn't violent enough. Ayers founded the Weather Underground, which carried out bombings just like McVeigh would do years later—and for similar reasons.

When Ayers almost got put away for his crimes, he decided he could do far more damage in the long term by becoming a college professor (see chapter 3). Ever since, Ayers has been hard at work encouraging his "students" to engage in violent protests. In the 1990s Ayers and Obama shared a business address in Chicago for at least three years. The extent of the relationship between the two men is shrouded in secrecy, but the elder Ayers clearly helped to mentor Obama.

It is no coincidence that left-wing violence increased dramatically on Obama's watch as President.

OCCUPY WALL STREET V. THE TEA PARTY

Throughout his presidency, Obama looked on in silence as left-wing mobs were created and allowed to flourish. After the out-of-control spending of the George W. Bush and Obama administrations, the Tea Party movement was born. It was an orderly, grassroots (naturally created) and constitutionally-based movement. In response, the Socialist, community-organizing left manufactured the Occupy Wall Street (OWS) movement (see chapter 11).

Ayers endorsed OWS. In one video, he is seen speaking to a group of them. Knowing that openly advocating violence would conflict with what the group was supposed to be about, Ayers told the group what he thought OWS should do instead:

"I think you should use your brilliance, your humor,
your wisdom, your body to dramatize the violence that exists."
– Bill Ayers, 2011

If you find yourself asking, "What does that even mean?" you're not alone.

Unlike the Tea Party movement, OWS had no real message, but it had plenty of angry welfare recipients. It consisted of a bunch of unproductive, spoiled, dirty miscreants who created a public nuisance in every city in which they set up camp. Disease and crime spread throughout many of these camps. Disorderly conduct became a regular occurrence. In one case, a woman who attended an OWS protest explained how dreadful things were inside the camp. In the interview, she explained how women were being groped and a deaf man raped.

Tea Party protesters were very orderly and respectful. Just check out the difference between how each group left the public property they used to protest:

Site of Tea Party Protest ending in 2009 (photo via Erin M, Flickr)

Site of Occupy Oakland (photo via Conservative Treehouse)

Oakland was a particularly bad location for the Occupy protests. Property damage, multiple injuries and at least one death was attributed to the lawless and violent movement. As for crime, no one seemed to do better at reporting it than OWS itself. The group launched a website that kept a running total of the number of arrests they had amassed. In 2016, the website proudly boasted there had been 7,775 arrests.

"HANDS UP, DON'T SHOOT"

In 2014, another left-wing movement was launched in the wake of the shooting of a black man named Michael Brown by a white police officer named Darren Wilson in Ferguson, Missouri. Witness accounts painted the picture of a lawless cop who murdered an innocent black man who had his hands up and was yelling, "Don't shoot!"

Riots ensued and a movement called *Black Lives Matter* (BLM) was born. They were fed by the Socialist mainstream media and organized by race hustlers. The money trail for *BLM* traced back to a very wealthy Socialist financier named George Soros.

As it turned out, the whole "Hands up, Don't Shoot" account never happened; it was a lie. That didn't stop the Socialists from pushing it to fuel their war with police. Wilson was found to be innocent. It was Brown who reached for Wilson's gun and had tried to harm the officer; the gun was fired inside the patrol car. Moments earlier, Brown committed shoplifting and shoved the clerk on his way out the door.

The more critical issue for the leaders of BLM was to cause chaos and attack the police who represented law and order. This is exactly what they did. There are several videos of the BLM protests and marches. In one, they can be seen threatening police. You can hear them shout, "PIGS IN A BLANKET! FRY 'EM LIKE BACON."

The truth is that BLM has nothing to do with a just response to racism. It's about community organizing, dividing people along racial lines, and agitation intended to bully and intimidate, just like Alinsky taught. BLM was racist toward Wilson, the smallest of minorities—the individual (see chapter 9).

The list of left-wing riots is endless. BLM and OWS are just two examples. There are several others but this is a short book.

Just challenge yourself to find incidents of public violence and riots that began because of a political issue. It is always either a left-wing Socialist group or an Islamic one (see chapter 19). That doesn't stop the Socialists from lying about who is committing the violence or blaming their law-abiding opponents for causing it.

CHAPTER 14

ABORT SOCIALISM

"We don't want the word to go out that
we want to exterminate the Negro population ... "
– Margaret Sanger, 1939

"The entire abortion industry is based on a lie."
– Norma McCorvey aka "Jane Roe" in Roe v. Wade

Margaret Sanger is considered the founder of Planned Parenthood (PP). Norma McCorvey was the "Jane Roe" in the *Roe v. Wade* Supreme Court case that legalized abortion in 1973 (without a law passed by Congress). McCorvey later had a major conversion and fought against abortion until her death.

Sanger began her outfit as a series of "birth control" clinics. In the more than 100 years since its founding, PP has "progressed" (there's that word again) to the mass genocide of infants.

Since the *Roe v. Wade* decision, there have been well over 50 million ~~abortions~~ murders. As a percentage, black babies are murdered at a much higher rate than any other race. There have been approximately 20 million black babies legally murdered since *Roe v. Wade,* but black females only make up 13 percent of the female population.

Yet, blacks support the Democrat Party to the tune of 90 percent. Guess who else does?

Planned Parenthood.

There is perhaps no better example of how successfully Socialists have deceived blacks into supporting them than the abortion issue (see chapter 10). Abortion defenders will say that the quote uttered by Sanger above is taken out of context, that she didn't mean what the quote seems to suggest. What Socialists cannot argue is that Sanger's legacy is precisely that—the extermination of blacks.

Consider that in 1926, Sanger delivered a rousing speech to the wives of the KKK in Trenton, New Jersey. She even wrote about the experience, saying that her words were extremely well received and that she wanted to speak to like-minded groups. When you put these things together, it points directly to Sanger wanting to exterminate blacks by murdering their babies.

Terms like "Planned Parenthood" and "Family Planning" sound great (that's what Socialists do with words) (see chapter 20). What the Socialists *won't* tell you is what they're *really* up to.

Just as "birth control" *progressed* to "abortion," so too has "abortion" *progressed* to "late-term abortion." It is now legal in some states to murder babies who have been in the womb for six months or more. With technology, babies born prematurely, well before that six-month mark, survive and live normal lives thanks to Neonatal Intensive Care Units (NICU).

In late-term abortions—also known as "partial birth abortions"—babies are *partially* born just before their brains are sucked out. The murdered baby is then disposed of—or its parts sold—and abortion "clinics" like PP move onto their next victims.

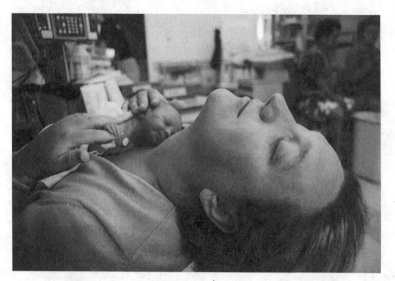

Mom and Premature Baby at Kapaiolani (photo via Wikipedia)

MONSTER

Perhaps the most horrifying case involving late-term abortions was that of Dr. Kermit Gosnell, a black man who ran a late term abortion clinic in Philadelphia. Most of Gosnell's victims were black women and their babies. Gosnell would use scissors to sever the spinal cord of babies who could have survived had they been born weeks or months earlier. In fact, Gosnell often performed these gruesome acts after delivering these babies alive.

Authorities were granted a warrant to search Gosnell's clinic over a matter involving the misuse of prescription drugs. What they found, they were not prepared for. There is a documentary video on the case, entitled, "3801 Lancaster," which can be viewed on *YouTube*. WARNING: GRAPHIC IMAGES AND DEPICTIONS.

Despite this decades-long holocaust on American soil, celebrities— including black ones—use their fame and influence to support abortion. Blacks who call Republicans racist support a group that is exterminat- ing ... blacks (see chapter 10). While doing a very un-funny skit, celebri- ties John Legend, St. Vincent and Zach Galifianakis promoted abortion for Planned Parenthood. In so doing, they performed a cover version of

"Loving You." Only Socialists would consider murder an act of love.

This is the legacy of Margaret Sanger and the *Roe v. Wade* decision. Fortunately, McCorvey had her eyes opened to the truth and fought for it vigorously. The key excerpt of her quote above is that she realized she was used and lied to.

That is Socialism.

WHY ABORTION GETS SO MUCH SUPPORT

Most of the abortion candidates are young women who aren't ready to be mothers, let alone *single* mothers. Socialists prey on this. After all, being a mother is very hard work. It takes tremendous love, sacrifice and responsibility. That is very scary to young teens who find themselves in this situation.

Is that the fault of the child?

No, but what abortion supporters will tell these young, scared, pregnant women is that it's not their fault either and that the baby is not a human being yet anyway. These young women are scared, too scared to understand that groups like PP are just plain evil. How much eviler can it get than to lie to a scared woman, murder her innocent baby, scar its mother for life, and then profit from it?

There are several undercover videos that have exposed the true intentions of PP. A quick *Google* search will reveal them.

It doesn't get more wicked and this is exactly the end-justifies-the-means mentality that Socialists thrive on.

Wicked Socialists convince these young women that abortion is just a form of birth control. What they *won't* tell these young women is that they need abortions to get paid—with taxpayer dollars and donations from people who watch videos like the one above. PP will insist that tax dollars are not used to fund abortions in their clinics, but that's a tough sell because abortions are what they're in business for. They have to lie about that too.

PP will tell you that abortions are a small percentage of what they do. They will tell you they also provide mammograms and cancer screenings to young women who couldn't otherwise get them.

Guess what? That's another lie and there are plenty of *YouTube* videos which demonstrate that as well.

Whenever abortion is debated in public forums, Socialists will always come back with, "Well, what about abortion in the case of rape and incest?" Unfortunately, the other side always gets sucked into that argument instead of putting it aside. Of all the abortions that take place, those involving rape and incest are an extremely small percentage—well below five percent. Debate the others, not the few that may or may not be justified.

Socialists know they can't justify murder, so they change the language (see chapter 20). PP President Cecile Richards pleaded for taxpayer dollars so that women could get mammograms. Again, that is a lie because PP doesn't do mammograms.

There is sex trafficking, racial extermination, murder, lies, the cover up of rape, the selling of baby parts, and so many more unspeakable crimes. All of this is the result of Socialism, which tells you that everyone must serve the common good. PP receives vast sums of taxpayer dollars to murder innocent babies and most taxpayers would object to their dollars being spent on such things.

It is Socialism that must be aborted.

CHAPTER 15

~~IMMIGRATION~~ INVASION

"Illegal Immigration is a crime, not a negotiation."
– Sheriff Joe Arpaio

When foreigners of any nation are allowed into that nation in large numbers, there is a reason. In America, Socialists want as many illegal aliens allowed in as possible. By appearing sympathetic to these aliens, Democrat Socialists can get their support—and eventually, their votes.

How?

By promising them the same things they promise their existing voters—free healthcare, free housing, free education, jobs, welfare, free this and free that. The elite globalist Socialists want illegal aliens in the U.S. because it makes them richer and more powerful through lower wages while weakening the middle class.

The laws that prevent illegal immigration are already in place. It's just that they haven't been enforced by those with the authority to do so.

They have their own Socialist reasons.

ILLEGAL ALIEN CRIMES

Crimes committed by illegal aliens in the U.S. (not including the crime of entering the country illegally) have skyrocketed in recent years. There have been deaths due to illegal aliens driving drunk. There have been rapes and assaults. There have been gruesome murders. Worse, in some cases, these crimes are committed by aliens who've already been deported multiple times.

Take the case of Kate Steinle. While walking on a pier in San Francisco with her father one evening, an illegal alien named Jose Inez Garcia Zarate fired a stolen gun three times. One of the bullets struck Steinle in the back. Two hours later, she was dead. Her killer had already been convicted of seven felonies and had been deported five times.

How Zarate came into possession of the gun was a subject of debate. That he did come into possession of it, was not. At his trial, Zarate faced a second-degree murder charge while being a felon in possession of a firearm and then using it. The jury also had the option of charging him with involuntary manslaughter, which simply means the death was caused by the reckless actions of the defendant.

Shockingly, the jury found Zarate not guilty on all charges of murder or manslaughter. The matter of his illegal alien status was not even considered.

A few months prior to Steinle's death, Zarate was in the San Francisco County Jail over an outstanding drug warrant. U.S. Immigrations and Customs Enforcement (ICE) requested that Zarate be detained until they could pick him up.

That didn't happen. The San Francisco Socialists released Zarate. Weeks later, Zarate would kill Kate Steinle.

In a sane world, public outrage would lead to the enforcement of immigration laws. In a country led by Socialists, the Socialist media (see chapter 8) all but ignores the story and the public is largely uninformed. When the matter is debated, Socialist politicians say it's unfair to label all illegal aliens as criminals because of the actions of a few.

Kate Steinle

What they will *not* acknowledge is that the failure to enforce immigration laws allows many more cases like this—far too many to chronicle in this book. The reason is that Socialists put power above country or its citizens.

Instead, if you object to illegal immigration, the Socialists will call you a racist or "xenophobic," which means you have an intense dislike for people from other countries. That's another Socialist lie because the truth is that Socialists who accuse patriots of xenophobia have an intense dislike for their *own* citizens. If they didn't, they would want to prevent more deaths, like Steinle's.

SANCTUARY CITIES

Socialists love to use effective words to push their lies (see chapter 20). One such word is "sanctuary." Sounds real nice, right? Sanctuary means things like asylum, immunity, protection, safety, refuge, or even a sacred place.

Using the logic of Socialists, however, the term Sanctuary City is used to describe a place where illegal aliens—who've already broken the law by entering the U.S. illegally—are given sanctuary from arrest or prosecution. Those Socialists also bank on most Americans not objecting to the term. Who would object to a term like Sanctuary City, right?

San Francisco, the city where Steinle was shot dead by an illegal alien, is one such city. As you can see, Socialists are interested in giving criminals sanctuary, not their own law-abiding citizens.

So, a sanctuary city is really all about your perspective. Only a Socialist would want to give criminals sanctuary and put their own citizens in danger.

The effectiveness of Socialist arguments like why illegal aliens should be allowed into the U.S. unchecked is because those arguments sound so sweet and look so good to bleeding heart liberals.

So does a cake filled with razor blades.

IMMIGRATION SYSTEM NOT BROKEN

Socialists will tell you that America's immigration system is broken. It's not. The people in charge of enforcing sound laws already on the books are what's broken. They're corrupt and driven only by their Socialist agenda. The immigration laws in this country are sound, but they're ignored. Instead, the Socialists will tell you we need "Comprehensive Immigration Reform."

Anytime you hear politicians say "comprehensive" anything, call them out. What they're really trying to do is to create a law so big that tax dollars can be hidden and then wasted in enormous amounts (see chapter 20). In the case of immigration, they want to protect criminals and welcome more of them.

All the while, they want you to believe that they're going to take your money and make you a Socialist utopia.

"A 'liberal paradise' would be a place where everybody has guaranteed employment, free comprehensive health care, free education, free food, free housing, free clothing, free utilities and only law enforcement personnel have guns.
And, believe it or not, such a liberal utopia does indeed exist ... It's called prison."
– Joe Arpaio

As former Sheriff of Maricopa County in Arizona, Sheriff Joe Arpaio fought Socialism and political correctness his entire career. He understood Socialism and he understood the games Socialists play. He also fought illegal immigration very hard. In one of his many quotes (above), he exposed the Socialist lie perfectly. In just those few words, he exposed how Socialists appeal to those whose support they want.

EUROPE'S IMMIGRATION PROBLEM

Most illegals flooding into the U.S. are Mexicans. Europe has itself an Islamic immigration problem. European leaders are truly playing with fire because the Islamic culture does not want Muslims to become a *part* of European culture. It wants conquest. As a result, there are so many enclaves in Europe known as "no-go zones" for police. As if that weren't bad enough, these Muslim invaders live off Socialist government programs like welfare and unemployment compensation.

Just as in the U.S., Europe is having to deal with illegal aliens who commit rape, assault, and murder. Any *YouTube* search will pull up dozens of videos of this problem.

The mastermind behind the 9/11 attacks, Khalid Sheikh Mohammed (KSM), was interviewed by a CIA contractor after his capture. Even the man behind the attack admitted that immigration was the best way for Islam to conquer America and Europe:

> *"(KSM said) ... the 'practical' way to defeat America was*
> *through immigration and by outbreeding non-Muslims."*
> *– CIA Contractor James Mitchell*

In 2013, a British Muslim of Nigerian descent murdered a British soldier with a meat cleaver in the street in broad daylight. The soldier, Lee Rigby, was walking across the street to a shop when the attack happened.

As conniving and clever as Socialists are, they're also very stupid. They fail to see that Socialism leads to their own destruction as well.

In 2011, European countries helped remove Muammar Gadhafi as leader of Libya, a Muslim North African country. Once Gadhafi was gone,

Europe had an instant refugee crisis to deal with. Civil war and unrest in Syria and Egypt also helped give Europe thousands of Muslim refugees.

European leaders welcomed invaders into their countries. As a result, they are proving KSM right. Islamic countries that seek to conquer non-Muslim countries have learned that by simply releasing thousands upon thousands of Muslims into countries who willingly accept them will lead to conquest (see chapter 19).

Again, Socialists are stupid.

SECTION IV

THE SOCIALIST ENDGAME

CHAPTER 16

RegYOUlated Militia

"A well regulated Militia, being necessary
to the security of a free State,
the right of the people to keep and bear Arms,
shall not be infringed."
– Second Amendment to U.S. Constitution

Whenever you engage a Socialist on the topic of gun control and the second amendment, he will inevitably point to the part about a "regulated militia" being the military, not you. If the military is regulated, what point is there for a citizen to have guns?

The point is that YOU are the militia.

As usual, Socialists do not understand why the U.S. Constitution was written. The "militia" was formed to fight an out-of-control government. America's founders realized this and wanted an armed citizenry to prevent it from happening again.

If you ever hear a debate on guns being about the right to hunt, you can shut it down easily. The second amendment has nothing to do with hunting. It has everything to do with stopping a corrupt government from employing the Castle Theory (see chapter 4).

Besides, if the military is "regulated," who regulates it, a neutral third party? No, those who seek power over you (see chapter 3). The government, which always becomes more corrupt and Socialist as it grows.

If the *government* is responsible for regulating the militia and the militia is "necessary to the security of a free State," how is a citizenry expected to protect itself from the same kind of tyrannical government that wants to *abolish* the free state? That's exactly why the Revolutionary War of 1776 was fought in the first place. It's also why the government wants to take away your guns, regardless of how crazy they say you are for believing it.

The truth is that the American citizens are *already* regulated far too much. In fact, if the second amendment were ever changed, "well regulated" would have to be replaced with "over regulated."

WOMAN FORCED TO WATCH HER PARENTS MURDERED

Consider the case of Suzanna Gratia-Hupp. In 1991, she went to lunch at a Luby's restaurant in Texas with her parents. While they were eating, a crazed man drove his vehicle through the window and into the restaurant. He then got out and began shooting random patrons at will.

Gratia-Hupp realized that she had left her gun in her car because before entering the restaurant, she decided to obey the law, which said it was a felony for her to carry a gun inside. When it was over, Suzanna's parents lay dead. She regretted *not breaking* that law.

Sometime later, she delivered emotional testimony to Congress.

The most powerful part of Suzanna's testimony came when she explained why the second amendment was in existence in the first place. While looking the congressmen in the eyes, Gratia-Hupp nailed it:

> *"The 2nd amendment is not about duck hunting ... it's about our rights ... to be able to protect ourselves from all of you guys up there."*
> *– Suzanna Gratia-Hupp*

The fact is that had Suzanna disobeyed the law, she would have been better prepared to save her parents' lives.

OPERATION FAST AND FURIOUS

Politicians who represent the Socialist state instead of the people will *always* support gun control. They will also tell you that's not true; they are lying. We just want "common sense" gun laws to protect citizens, they say. Whenever you hear that, the politician is lying to you (that shouldn't be a shock; lying comes easy to politicians). What he really means is that he wants common sense laws to protect the government from the Constitution.

The truth is that there is no shortage of gun laws. In fact, there are so many of them on the books that they can't all be enforced. That never stops Socialists. The next time there is a mass shooting, take note of how many politicians call for the enforcement of existing gun laws.

You'll never get out of single digits.

What you *will* find is that the Socialist gun-grabbers will always call for *stricter* laws. They do this because it inches them closer and closer to taking them from you.

Sometimes, it's much worse than that. In 2009, the Bureau of Alcohol, Tobacco and Firearms (ATF) under the Obama administration, instructed gun store owners to sell guns to criminals against the will of those store owners. Why?

The ATF—under the Obama administration—knew that those guns would end up in the hands of Mexican drug cartels; that was the plan. Those cartels would use those guns to murder innocent people. When the guns found at the crime scenes were traced back to American gun store owners, politicians could push for stricter gun control laws. After all, guns sold in America were being used to murder innocent people in a foreign country.

When one of the guns was found at the murder scene of U.S. Border Patrol Agent Brian Terry, the operation was exposed. Terry did not die in vain but neither was justice served. When the operation was exposed, thousands of weapons had ended up in the hands of those cartels. The death toll continues to climb and will for years to come.

The number of murders will never be known, but the reason for the operation is—for those willing to admit it. The corrupt administration of a Socialist president thought innocent deaths were a small price to pay for taking guns away from Americans

Border Patrol Agent Brian Terry (Photo via Brian Terry Foundation)

When ATF whistleblower Agent John Dodson confronted his supervisor about the immoral operation, he was told the following:

> *"If you're going to make an omelet,*
> *you've got to scramble some eggs."*
> *– ATF Supervisor David Voth*

Of course, the omelet Voth was referring to was the confiscation of guns. One of the "eggs" ended up being Terry. The moral of this story is, don't be an egghead. Resist gun control because it's not about controlling guns; it's about confiscating *them* and controlling *you*.

Operation Fast and Furious proved it.

GUN OWNERSHIP IS PATRIOTIC

In a more positive, patriotic light is the necessity to bear arms because it enlists every American household into a *domestic* militia in the event of any invasion, mass disturbance, or even the recent craze of preparation for the zombie apocalypse. OK, that's over the edge ... even for us! But look at events such as Hurricane Katrina or other situations where the social services break down. During extreme events, it is every man for himself. If you had to protect your family in the middle of that chaos, you want to be trained and packing heat to deter would-be assailants from choosing your family.

Following our laws, respecting others, and getting trained with a firearm is how to ensure personal safety on your next successful hunt, range competition, or self-defense encounter.

Most bad gun-related incidents are caused by those untrained and without the legal right to possess. They tend to choose locations where the right to bear arms has been infringed upon, which is why crazy mass-shooters usually choose venues like schools, universities, shopping malls and ... restaurants to wreak their carnage. They know they have a captive, unarmed audience with the luxury of tens of minutes before any armed response arrives. These cowards only go where people are known to have willfully given up their rights.

"Gun-Free Zones" are a sick joke created by Socialist gun-grabbers. After all, nothing is more welcoming to a criminal with a gun than a place where there are innocent people and *no* guns. Leave it up to Socialists to think that criminals obey the law.

Think about it. If you're in a restaurant and a gunman shows up and starts randomly shooting patrons, wouldn't you like to have a law-abiding citizen in there with a gun (assuming you don't have one)?

Suzanna Gratia-Hupp is a law-abiding citizen who wishes she'd have broken a stupid law.

Finally, the simplest argument for gun ownership is that if citizens are not armed, the only ones *with* the guns would be the criminals and the police.

As they say, when seconds count, the police are minutes away.

Our men and women in uniform do their best; we greatly respect and appreciate them. Not everyone is comfortable with owning a gun and there is nothing wrong with that. That doesn't mean you shouldn't support the right of others who are willing and able to own that gun.

Just remember: the protection of your loved ones is ultimately *your* responsibility, not the government's.

YOU are the RegYOUlated militia and don't let anyone tell *you* any different.

CHAPTER 17

CLIMATE CHANGE CONSPIRACY

"The entire North Polarized cap will disappear in 5 years."
– Al Gore in 2008

While speaking in Germany in December of 2008, former Vice President Al Gore stated that the North Pole would disappear in five years. Not only has that five years come and gone, but the North Pole has expanded since then.

In 2009, Gore gave testimony to Congress urging it to act on global warming. As he did so, snow blanketed the Nation's Capital outside. In other testimony, Gore insisted, "The earth has a fever!"

When inconvenient weather events became too much to bear, the term Global Warming was replaced with Climate Change.

If there is one trait that Socialists like Gore have in abundance, it's the inability to feel shame—the absence of conscience. Instead of acknowledging his exposed lies, Gore just kept on going.

The argument from those chicken littles about climate change is that mankind is contributing to it and that it's leading to the end of the world.

In fact, there is no evidence to support that; it's all manufactured to push a fraud scheme to—you guessed it—take your money.

Like Socialists who pushed for Social Security, Medicare and Medicaid, those who want you to believe in Anthropogenic (man-made) Climate Change are simply using that as an excuse to steal from you and enrich themselves.

"How?" you ask.

Simple. Man-made Climate Change believers (MMCCB) tell you that the release of Carbon Dioxide ($CO2$) into the air causes a "Greenhouse Effect." In Greenhouses, many of the sun's rays can enter a greenhouse, but are absorbed and cannot *exit*; this causes the temperature inside to rise.

What the MMCCBs want you to believe is that you need to reduce your "Carbon Footprint" (the amount of $CO2$ you use or expel into the atmosphere). What this means is that you are supposed to drive your car less (or get a smaller one), keep your lights off, watch less television, use your iPhone less, use less air conditioning in the summer, go without heat in the winter, etc. While you're at it, you might want to try breathing less than you do now because when you exhale, you emit $CO2$—which plants, by the way love (plants and trees inhale $CO2$ and exhale oxygen; we humans do the opposite). If the ever-so-earth-friendly, tree-hugging Socialists really cared about plants, they would plant more of them so that they could consume more $CO2$. Instead, they want *you* to breathe less, which only harms the environment because trees have less $CO2$ to inhale.

In 2007, scientists discovered that the average temperature on earth's surface had been increasing by the same amount as the average temperature on the surface of Mars' had been. How could this be? Mars is uninhabited (we think) so how could global warming be happening there because of human activity? The answer is *not* Martian activity.

There is one variable that affects both Earth and Mars—the Sun. It is the Sun which has a far greater impact on the earth's climate than anything man might be doing.

Aside from MMCCBs telling you that humans—simply by living— are destroying the planet, the leaders of the Climate Change fraud have huge Carbon Footprints. Gore and the Hollywood celebrities who fawn over him have their own private planes and huge homes.

They will tell you that they need these things to do the work of alarming everyone. It's just a necessary cost of ~~doing business~~ committing fraud.

Ah, the hypocrisy of, "Do as I say, not as I do" couldn't be more obvious.

CAP AND TRADE

Leaders of the MMCCB seek to get rich. They want to "cap" the amount of CO2 that you're allowed to use. If you use less than what is allowed by law, you would get "carbon credits," which you could then "trade" with someone who used more than his or her quota. If you can't find someone to trade with, you'd have to pay a fine. Of course, someone would have to manage all of this, right?

Guess who?

That's right, the Socialists in government. In the name of helping people, those sick leeches are simply looking to take your money. Sound familiar?

Fortunately, attempts by the Obama administration to ram this legislation down the throats of the American people was not successful. Like Obamacare, it was fraud disguised as a way to help people.

Those of us who disagree with the need for Cap and Trade are called "climate deniers" who refuse to look at the "consensus" of scientists. For one thing, science is not about "consensus." It's about verifiable and provable facts.

If science *were* about "consensus," 2+2=5 would become true if enough scientists said that it is. Anyone who disagreed would be labeled a math denier.

What the Socialist media will *not* tell you is that there is a very simple reason why so many "scientists" push for this kind of consensus. That reason is that they're rewarded with government grants if they push the lie. That's right, scientists were being bribed and bought to betray their own professions. The corrupt Socialists in government—as well as lobbyists—have been pushing this fraud and can certainly part with millions of taxpayer dollars if it means getting scientists to help with the fraud. After all, it's not really their money, anyway, right?

GREEN TECHNOLOGY

Another place the climate change agenda reared its head was in the formation of "green technology" companies. They had no chance of surviving without taxpayer money flowing in. Once these companies—like Solyndra—were founded, the money managers of politicians invested in them. When they did, the money flowed in and the stocks shot up hundreds of percent. The money managers raked in the cash, getting huge profits just before the companies collapsed.

It was nothing short of possibly the biggest boondoggle in the history of the world. Of course, the Socialist media didn't care. After all, their agenda is the same as the Socialists who run this scam (see chapter 8).

This is known as crony Capitalism, which is the same as Socialism. When crooked politicians profit from taxpayer-funded programs, it's criminal; it's fraud and grand larceny. If you or anyone of us did the same thing, we'd be sitting in prison today.

How does that sound when you listen to the Socialists tell you that we need Socialism so that everyone is equal (see chapter 3)?

CLIMATEGATE

A scandal that broke in 2009 revealed exactly what the MMCCBs were up to; that scandal exposed their lies.

As the world's elitists were salivating over the prospect of Cap and Trade under a new Obama administration, they were preparing to attend the Climate Change Summit in Copenhagen, Denmark when disaster (for them) struck. A computer server at the Climate Research Unit (CRU) located at East Anglia University in Great Britain was hacked. Thousands upon thousands of emails were then released to the public.

In the wake of the scandal, Summit attendees arrived in Copenhagen just in time for a snow storm.

What the emails showed was that Climate Change "scientists" were actually manipulating data (lying again) to fit their arguments. They were also intimidating lower level scientists to get on board. Emails revealed that those who wouldn't play along were mocked and ridiculed.

Among all the emails, graphs, claims, and fraudulent activity that were exposed, there was one chart that stood out above all the others. It's known as the "hockey stick" chart because it showed several hundred years of declining temperatures and then a sudden jump at about the time of increased CO_2 emissions at the beginning of the 20th century and continues to go up. The emails also revealed that crucial data was intentionally left out to create the "hockey stick" and present it as scientific fact.

The man behind the "hockey stick" was Michael Mann of Penn State University. Adding to the damage was the fact that vice president Gore had used Mann's "hockey stick" as a central component in his 2006 book and movie entitled, "An Inconvenient Truth." In other words, Gore's work is all based on a lie, which makes *it* invalid and Gore a fraud.

Political commentator Mark Steyn, who was sued by Mann in 2012 for defamation, had been a critic of the "hockey stick" since 2001. During a 2015 speech, Steyn concluded with a very succinct and spot-on assessment:

"Climate science (must) recover its integrity and climb off the hockey stick."
– Mark Steyn

The Climate Change movement has its leaders, its operatives, and its staunch, blind believers who just go along. Gore represents the leadership, Mann represents the operatives and those who believe it all are the useful idiots, a term said to have been coined by Vladimir Lenin (see chapter 3).

A useful idiot is someone who blindly follows a leader without fully understanding the beliefs or objectives of that leader. When it comes to Climate Change, the useful idiots are the ones who prevent people like Gore and Mann from suffering the consequences of their fraudulent activity.

Perhaps Reagan said it best:

"The problem with our liberal (Socialist) friends is not that they're ignorant. It's just that they know so much that isn't so."
– Ronald Reagan

Unfortunately, whether it's ignorance or deceit, MMCCBs are using a Socialist tactic to push a Socialist agenda.

CHAPTER 18

GLOBALISM IS SOCIALISM

"I'm glad to sit at the right hand of Satan."
– Walter Cronkite

If you're asking yourself why so many Socialists seem to revere Satan, you're asking the right questions. There was a time when Walter Cronkite was known as "the most trusted man in America" (see chapter 8). In a pre-internet age, millions of Americans relied on him to deliver the news from their television sets. The truth is that Cronkite was never objective; he was deceitful.

In 1999, while accepting the Norman Cousins Global Governance Award from the World Federalist Association, Cronkite expressed loyalty to the devil. Cronkite did so after quoting Christian televangelist Pat Robertson, who had written that there should be no world government until "the Messiah" arrives. This was clearly a reference to the second coming of Jesus.

Cronkite then proceeded to mock that notion by expressing loyalty to the devil himself.

Cronkite was a globalist and believed in placing the power to rule the world into the hands of an elite few. If that sounds like a much larger version of Castle Theory, it is (see chapter 4).

Something else Cronkite said in that video is that America would have to "yield up some ... sovereignty."

What is sovereignty?

In short, it's defined as:

> *"The quality or state of being sovereign,*
> *or of having supreme power or authority."*

Sovereignty can exist at the individual level, when you have supreme power over yourself (freedom) or it can exist on a global level, which would be extremely dangerous. Our country's Declaration of Independence acknowledges that the sovereignty of an individual was granted by God and that each person is, "endowed by their Creator" *with* that sovereignty (see chapter 9).

Sovereignty can also exist on a national level. The United States is a sovereign nation that has power over itself. What makes it unique, however, is that the founding documents (primarily the Bill of Rights) were written based on every citizen having rights given by God that guarantee *individual* sovereignty.

This is what drives Socialists crazy; they hate that.

They want the U.S. to give up its sovereignty to the United Nations. Doing so would guarantee the loss not only of America's sovereignty but that of each of its citizens.

That is what Socialism wants.

EUROPEAN UNION

Look at the European Union to see a window into global government. It was billed as an attempt to unite Europe and thereby make the lives of its inhabitants easier by doing things like abolishing the need for passports. The problem—as is with all things Socialist—is that power and sovereignty was surrendered to a much smaller group of people who were as equally arrogant as they were incompetent.

Fortunately, there were a few voices of reason (actually, VERY few) within the EU. One such voice was Britain's Nigel Farage, a Member of European Parliament (MEP), who understood perfectly the globalist nature of the EU. In a video from 2010, Farage stood up and explained how the EU's roots are in communism.

In another video from 2010, Farage confronted Herman Van Rompuy, the President of the European Council at the time, to his face. Among other things, Farage said the following directly to Van Rompuy:

> *"You have the charisma of a damp rag and*
> *the appearance of a low-grade bank clerk."*
> *– Nigel Farage*

The videos of Farage are endless, but another is from way back in 2005. In it, Farage confronts British Prime Minister at the time, Tony Blair. Blair was a huge supporter of the EU and shared the same globalist, elitist, and Socialist views of how the world should be. Farage called him out for his socialist agenda.

In 2016, Great Britain's people voted to leave the EU. The vote—billed as "Brexit"—sent shockwaves across the world. In the end, Farage was credited with being a key player in helping "Brexit" become a reality.

There were many factors that led to the British people voting to leave the EU, but chief among them was the mass immigration of Muslims into Europe from places like Syria and Pakistan (see chapter 15). As is the case with Socialists, there was little regard for the safety and sovereignty of its people.

Political leaders ignored the consequences of this mass immigration invasion. Those consequences included heinous crimes like rape, assault, and murder. This says nothing of these Muslims getting government benefits like ... wait for it ... welfare and unemployment pay.

Most dangerous to Europe are the intentions of the Islamic world. The leaders of Islam seek to abolish national borders, just as the EU sought to do (see chapter 19). However, Islam seeks to replace those borders with a global government that rules by Islamic Law. Socialists think that's just fine ... until they are ruled by it.

CHAPTER 19

SOCIAL-ISLAM

"(Islam) increases, instead of lessening, the fury of intolerance."
— Sir Winston Churchill

"(Islam) too would have been more compatible
to us than Christianity."
— Adolph Hitler

Perhaps no two men represent the sides of good and evil in World War II better than British Prime Minister Winston Churchill and Nazi Socialist Adolph Hitler. Earlier in his career, Churchill learned a great deal about Islam; he rejected it. Hitler, however, aligned with the Muslim Brotherhood during the war.

After all, the Nazis and the Muslims had a common enemy—the Jews.

Islam and Socialism have very much in common as well. Both reject Christianity; both seek blind and loyal subjects; both are intolerant of opposing views; both have a past that includes slavery (Islam still practices it); both rule by fear and oppression; both have a history of mass genocide; and both seek global domination.

ISLAMIC CALIPHATE

Globalism is the goal of Socialists. Social Security, Medicare, Medicaid, Obamacare and Climate Change propaganda are all just vehicles they use to get there. Globalism is also the goal of Islam.

The Islamic world seeks what is called a global Caliphate.

What is a Caliphate?

It is a system of government ruled over by a Caliph or Muslim King who enforces strict Islamic law (Sharia). Sharia law cannot co-exist with the U.S. Constitution, for example. The first amendment to the Constitution protects freedoms of religion, speech, and petitioning the government. Sharia law prohibits all of that. Non-Muslims are persecuted and speech against Islam or an Islamic government is considered a capital offense, punishable by death.

For example, there are no churches or synagogues in Saudi Arabia, only mosques.

Islam seeks to eliminate national borders and rule the world according to Sharia Law. There once was a Caliphate known as the Ottoman Empire, which was based in what is today, Turkey. It was abolished after World War I, but the Muslim world has been pushing for its re-birth ever since. Just as Socialists do, Muslim leaders will lie about their intentions.

There are Muslim groups in the U.S. that are pushing for this. Groups like the Council on American-Islamic Relations (CAIR), the Islamic Society of North America (ISNA), the Muslim Students Association (MSA) and many others are all part of the Muslim Brotherhood, which is pushing for the overthrow of the American system of government, regardless of what they or the Socialist media says (see chapter 8).

Perhaps it's no coincidence at all that the best non-Muslim allies the Muslims have are the Socialists, and for good reason.

Both are comprised of—and depend on—liars and useful idiots.

INFILTRATION

The Muslim Brotherhood's operation in America really began to take root over half a century ago. It's a very stealth movement that has made tremendous strides. Members of this movement have had the most success by finding common cause with Socialist Democrats.

In 2006, Keith Ellison became the first Muslim elected to the U.S. Congress. In 2008, Andre Carson became the second. Both men are Democrats and both men belong to the Democratic Socialists of America (DSA) caucus. Ellison has been found to have very close ties to the Muslim Brotherhood groups in the U.S. There are questionable ties that link him to Hamas, an officially designated terrorist group.

Even two-time presidential candidate Hillary Clinton—a Socialist by any measure—has had a Muslim Brotherhood operative at her side for decades now. In 2011, Huma Abedin—Hillary's Deputy Chief of Staff—was publicly outed for her extensive familial ties to the group. A year later, five members of Congress brought it into a bigger spotlight. Ellison was the first prominent figure to come to her defense.

In 2004, thanks to a traffic stop in Maryland, the residence of a Muslim man with outstanding warrants was raided by the FBI. In that home, the FBI recovered several boxes of documents. One of those documents is dated May 19, 1991. Known as the *Explanatory Memorandum* for the Muslim Brotherhood's plan to destroy America, the document clearly explains how it will be done.

> *"(the Muslim Brotherhood in America) ...*
> *presents Islam as a civilization alternative,*
> *and supports the global Islamic State wherever it is."*
> *– Explanatory Memorandum, 1991, emphasis added.*

That term "global" is music to the ears of Socialist Democrats. The author of the memorandum also explained the Brotherhood's goal:

> *"(the Muslim Brotherhood's) work in America is*

a kind of grand jihad in eliminating and destroying
the western civilization from within and 'sabotaging'
its miserable house by their hands and the hands of (Muslims) ... "
– Explanatory Memorandum, 1991

Any American should be outraged by this. It's largely ignored by Democrats. That is because Socialists view patriotic Americans as an enemy they can defeat by being allies with the Islamic enemies of America.

CHAPTER 20

WAR WITH WORDS

"Political language ... is designed to make lies sound truthful and murder respectable, and to give an appearance of solidity to pure wind."
– George Orwell

George Orwell, author of many famous books, foresaw the whole movement of "political correctness" for what it was—thought control. He saw precisely how the powers that desired Socialism would use language to hide the ugly policies they hoped would take root and grow over the years. Just think about the term itself. "Politically correct" sounds so nice doesn't it? Who could argue with something that is non-offensive to anyone, right?

There's a slight problem. That's not what "politically correct" means. What it *means* is thought control. In Orwell's book, *1984* there were actual Thought Police who enforced it. In our society, the Socialists would love to use actual thought police. Instead, they use the public square at every opportunity. The funny thing is, though, that "political correctness" only has as much validity as people are willing to give it. We pride ourselves on being actively, politically *in*correct. It is so much more intellectually liberating to say what you think rather than let other people dictate how you should think and express yourself.

Typically, when you hear the phrase, "war of words," you think of a verbal argument. However, in the case of Socialists, words are used as weapons to defeat the other side before any debate takes place. For years, Socialists have used these words to hide their true intentions and to corrupt the true meaning of those words. This chapter is intended to help you identify and expose these tactics.

Below is a list of some examples:

1. Abortion – There was a time when the word "abort" simply meant to cease an activity or a mission. Today, its first meaning in the dictionary is "to bring forth a fetus from the uterus before the fetus is viable." That sounds harmless, doesn't it? Far from it. It's murder but the left has successfully changed the language from murder to abortion.

2. Affirmative Action – Two very powerful words, right? "Affirmative" means yes. To "affirm" is to confirm that something is true. "Action" means getting something done. So if you are affirming that something is true and then acting to make sure it happens, who would be against that? Well, again Socialists intentionally corrupt the meaning of words. The true meaning of affirmative action is reverse racial discrimination. It mandated that employers hire a certain number of minority candidates, regardless of qualification. If that sounds like negative action to you, you're thinking clearly.

3. Assault Weapons – This is a term used by Socialists who want to remove guns from citizens. The term "assault" is a negative word. The term means committing unlawful physical harm or committing a physical attack on someone. A weapon is something used to carry out an assault or to cause great harm *during* an assault. Semi-automatic weapons like the AK-47 are classified as assault weapons by Socialists. The word "assault," when tied to a weapon, implies that the weapon itself is responsible for any action it is used to commit. This is intended to make guns bad, not the bad people who use them in the commissions of crime. If people see the gun as something bad, Socialists know that those guns can be taken away more easily.

4. Comprehensive (Fill in the blank) Reform – The Socialist left loves to put key terms in between these two words. Take your pick, whether it's Comprehensive Immigration Reform or Comprehensive Healthcare Reform, the intent is simple but deceptive. The term "comprehensive" means a whole bunch of things are going to get fixed. "Reform" means they're going to get fixed right. The truth is that the fix is in. Whenever you hear Socialists talk about comprehensive anything, run. If they get their way, they'll steal Americans' wealth and waste it while enriching themselves and making things worse.

5. Discrimination – This term has successfully been changed by leftists to mean something negative. It used to be that to discriminate meant to use discretion or to make decisions and value judgments based on reason. Today, it is synonymous with racism. It's gotten to the point that if you're told you're discriminating, you're being a racist.

6. Forward – Socialists love this word. By saying they want to "move forward," they're really saying that their opponents want to go backward or remain stuck in the past. The truth is that Socialists just want to move *Socialism* forward, which only leads to hell. After all, criminals always move "forward" when committing crimes. Don't armed robbers "move forward" when they walk into a liquor store with a loaded gun? Don't they "move forward" when taking a hostage or pulling the trigger?

7. Inter-Faith Dialogue – This is a favorite of stealth Muslim Brotherhood jihadists. Any criticism of Islam is deemed to be religious discrimination. Muslim community leaders portray themselves as being open by seeking out relationships with people of other faiths like Christianity and Judaism. It's all a ruse. They seek to shut down criticism of Islam while creating the perception that they are open minded.

8. (Fill in the blank)-Phobia – In the twisted minds of the 21st century Socialists, the word "phobia" no longer means what the dictionary says it means. The true meaning of any phobia is an "irrational fear," like a fear of heights (acrophobia) or fear of being closed in (claustrophobia). Note that such fears only involve one individual—the person with the fear. However, the left has taken the word "phobia" and changed it to mean that the person or group who has the condition is racist for having it. Some examples include Islamophobia (irrational fear of Islam); homophobia (irrational fear of homosexuality); and xenophobia (irrational fear of illegal aliens). The only cure for these "phobias" is to accept Islam, homosexuality, and illegal aliens. It's a "heads I win, tails you lose" tactic. In short, you are a racist if you disagree. If you agree, you're cool. Yes, Socialists have taken the word "phobia" and made racists out of the people they say have these phobias. That's how you can tell if a phobia is really a *fauxbia*. If the source of the so-called fear is a certain group of people, you can bet it's the Socialists on the left who came up with it.

9. Planned Parenthood – Doesn't "parenthood" sound like a good word? It is. To "plan" something is good too, right? It means that you're taking control of something, that you're looking ahead, that you're thinking about the future and acting accordingly. It requires discipline and forethought. Put the two words together and you have the largest mass murder outfit in the United States. What this organization does is help young women who—in most cases—fail to plan. PP then convinces these women to let them murder their unborn children and call it "parenthood."

10. Pro-Choice – Only Socialists can get away with using words to make the mass murder of babies sound good. The word "choice" implies freedom. If everyone has a "choice," everyone is free to choose, right? Who couldn't argue with that? That's what putting the term "pro" in front does. Having a choice isn't good or bad. It's about how and what you choose. If choosing by itself is good, there would be no need for crime laws. When people choose to commit crimes, there are consequences for doing so. In the case of abortion (murder), Socialists have managed to change the language so that a woman can simply choose to have her unborn baby ripped from her and disposed of, without consequences.

11. Progressive – A word Socialists love to use to describe themselves.

In the late 1800s, they argued that "progress" would happen when the rich were made less rich so that the poor could be made richer (See Ten Cannots in Chapter 11). This was about wealth re-distribution which, as we know, is about Socialists taking their cut and everyone else suffering. Progress is a positive sounding word that implies moving forward or improving. Well, it *is* about moving forward, but it's about moving forward down the road to hell, which *is* downhill.

12. Rights (Civil, Women's, Minority, Voting et al.) – Who doesn't want rights? Who would be so evil as to deny someone's rights? That is precisely why the left loves this word. If a black person is arrested, his civil rights are violated. If a woman is prevented from murdering her unborn child, her "reproductive" rights are violated. If someone who is not legally registered to vote is told he/she can't vote, voting rights are being violated. Each one of those individuals did something wrong or illegal. The Socialist would have you believe that preventing or confronting such behavior violates the rights of an entire group of people.

13. Sanctuary City – This may be the most effective and devious of Socialist terms. The word "Sanctuary" is very positive sounding. Who wouldn't like to go to a city that is a "sanctuary"? Once again, it's a complete misuse of the term. As the Socialists define it, a sanctuary city is one in which criminals (illegal aliens) can be free from arrest or deportation. It's the law-abiding citizens who suffer. It is *their* city that becomes less safe when Socialists grant sanctuary to criminals. If you object, you're Xenophobic.

14. Undocumented Immigrant – It used to be that when a foreigner illegally entered the U.S. the term used to describe such a person was, "illegal alien." Today, the term "illegal" has been replaced by "undocumented" and "alien" with "immigrant." Since America is a country founded on immigrants (Socialists love making that point), we are supposed to sympathize with lawbreakers. The reason Socialists want more illegal aliens in the U.S. is because they know the clear majority of them can be fooled into becoming Democrat voters. Once again, it's all about power—at the expense of the country.

These are but a few examples but you get the point. Anytime a Socialist, Democrat, Leftist, or big government supporter uses positive sounding words, question it. Why was such a word chosen? What's the true intent? What is the objective?

Socialists are extremely effective because they know how to manipulate language to make their own evil intentions sound good. If you can spot those intentions and challenge them, you are ahead of the game. The Socialist endgame requires you not to notice.

Hopefully, this book can help you to see through this evil because, after all ...

Socialism Sucks ... Your Money from YOUR Pocket.